HOW TO BECOME THE HAPPIEST MUSLIM WOMAN ON EARTH

WRITTEN BY
DR. 'A'ID AL-QARNI

PUBLISHED BY
AL-FIRDOUS – LONDON

First Edition: 2006

Typeset by Abu Ruqayah
Cover Design by Halil Ozturk

ISBN 1 874263 98 1

Published and Distributed by:
Al-Firdous Ltd.
10 Fonthill Road
London N4 3 HX
www.al-firdous.com

Printed in England by De-Luxe Printers Ltd.
245a, Acton Lane, London NW10 7NR
email: deluxeprinters1@aol.com
Tel: 020 8965 1771

Table of Contents

Dedication

To every Muslim woman who accepts Allah ﷻ as her Lord, Islam as her religion and Muhammad as her Prophet.

To every girl who follows the path of Truth and carries the Message of Truthfulness.

To every teacher who strives with her words, observes her values and has purified her soul.

To every mother who brings her children up to be mindful of Allah ﷻ, to follow the Sunnah of His Messenger, and to love moral excellence.

I call on every anxious and sad woman to expect cheerfully a happy ending in the Care of Allah ﷻ, with great rewards and expiation of sins.

Introduction

Praise to Allah ﷻ, the Lord of the Worlds, and prayers and peace be upon the Messenger of Allah, his family, his companions and those who followed him.

This book implores the Muslim woman to be pleased with her religion, to enjoy Allah's Grace upon her and take pleasure in the blessings bestowed upon her. This book is a sign of hope and glad tidings to every woman whose heart has been depressed and her worries increased. It urges her to look forward to ease after hardship; it addresses her purified soul, her chaste heart and her pure spirit and says to her: be patient and anticipate your reward from Allah ﷻ; do not lose hope or despair of the Mercy of Allah ﷻ; be optimistic, for Allah ﷻ is with you; He ﷻ is All-Sufficient for you; He ﷻ is your only Protector and Supporter.

Dear sister, read this book where you will find clear Verses of the Qur'an, true Hadiths, inspiring stories, sound ideas and rightly guided experiences. Read this book in order to chase away all your worries and concerns. Study its volumes to help you cleanse your mind from all aspects of illusions and devilish whispers. This book will rather guide you towards the gardens of happiness and the land of faith, in the hope that Allah ﷻ makes you happy both in this life and in the Hereafter.

I have made this book like a jewel with which to adorn yourself. If you possess this book, then you would not care about all the jewellery in the world or any other types of adornments, for they are merely a frivolous waste fashion. Adorn yourself with the message of this book; wear it in any life festival, in cheerful events and ceremonies so that you will be – if Allah wills – the happiest woman in this world.

The way to your happiness depends on the purity of your knowledge and culture, and this is not attained by reading romantic fiction, which draws the reader outside her real world. You may find in these fictional stories some dramatic dreams and illusions, but they cause frustration and make the soul suffer a killing depression. The stories of Agatha Christie, for example, teach betrayal, crime and theft. I have read the series of Great World Fiction, which are a selection of the most attractive Nobel Prize-winning stories, and found them carrying serious mistakes and foolish ideas; however, there are still some good stories in the series, with a high standard of artistic narration, such as "The Old Man and the Sea" by Earnest Hemingway and other stories, which avoid immorality and indecency and were free of any low ethical standards.

It is the responsibility of every Muslim woman to read only the rightly guided books, such as the writings of Al-Tantawi, Al-Kilani, Al-Manfaluti, Al-Rafi'i, etc, their work was clean; their conscience was pure and they carried a clear message. I have mentioned this point, because I was keen about the purity of my work from the blemish of the foreign influence and the deviation of the corrupt.

In any case, there is nothing more exalted or perfect than the stories mentioned by Allah ﷻ in His Book (the Qur'an) or the Prophet ﷺ in his Sunnah (Traditions), and the great history of the rightly guided Caliphs, scholars and pious people. Enjoy the Grace of Allah ﷻ, for you are the happiest woman in the world as you follow the Religion of Islam, which is the true guidance.

By Dr. 'A'id al-Qarni

CHAPTER 1

Welcome!

Welcome to you as you pray, fast and supplicate submissively.

Welcome to you as you observe the Hijab with modesty and gravity.

Welcome to you as you are educated, aware and rightly guided.

Welcome to you as you are faithful, loyal, truthful and generous.

Welcome to you as you are patient, repentant and charitable.

Welcome to you as you remember Allah ﷻ with gratitude.

Welcome to you as you are a follower of Asiyah, Maryam and Khadijah.

Welcome to you as you raise heroes and produce men.

Welcome to you as you observe values and ethics.

Welcome to you as you guard the sacrosanct and keep away from prohibitions.

YES!

Yes to your beautiful smile, which sends out love and friendship to others.

Yes to your good word, which builds lawful friendships and eliminates hatred.

Yes to an accepted charity, which cheers the destitute and satisfies the hungry.

Yes to a session of Qur'an recitation with understanding and practice upon its meaning.

Yes to countless supplications seeking Allah's Forgiveness with true repentance.

Yes to raising your children in Islam, teaching them the Sunnah with right guidance.

Yes to observing modesty as commanded by Allah ﷻ to safeguard your dignity.

Yes to the company of pious Muslim women who fear Allah ﷻ, love Islam and observe its teachings.

Yes to piety towards the parents, keeping good kinship, honouring the neighbours and caring for orphans.

Yes to good education and useful reading of beneficial books.

NO!

No to wasting of one's life in trivialities, such as seeking revenge from others or indulging in irrelevant arguments.

No to the preference of accumulating wealth over one's health, happiness, rest and peace of mind.

No to the focus on other people's mistakes and backbiting about them, while forgetting one's faults.

No to indulging in satisfying one's whims and low desires.

No to wasting of one's time with idle people and spending hours in fooling around.

No to neglecting one's body and home in terms of purity and order.

No to consuming prohibited alcoholic drinks and smoking.

No to carelessness about the Hereafter and working towards it.

No to wasting one's wealth in prohibited activities or in excess of lawful ones.

Words of reflection

1- Remember that your Lord forgives those who seek forgiveness, and accepts the repentance of those who repent to Him sincerely.

2- Be merciful towards the weak and you will enjoy happiness. Be generous towards the destitute and you will be well. Do not carry hatred inside and you will be safe.

3- Be optimistic, for Allah ﷻ is with you, the angels call for forgiveness for you, while Paradise awaits you.

4- Wipe away your tears by having good thoughts of your Lord, and chase away your worries by remembering Allah's Blessings upon you.

5- Do not think that this world is ever perfect for anyone, for there is no one on earth who has fulfilled all her desires or is free from any grief or distress.

6- Be high-minded like a palm tree; when stones are thrown at it, it throws back its fruits.

7- Have you ever heard that sorrow brings back what has gone and that grief sets right any mistake? So why grieve and worry then?

8- Do not anticipate trouble and hardship; rather expect peace and safety and good health, if Allah wills.

9- Extinguish the flames of hatred in your breast with a general amnesty to all those who mistreated you.

10- Remember that body washing, ablution, fragrance, siwak and life order are successful treatments for every distress and grief.

Words of reflection

1- Be like a bee; it falls only on fragrant roses and fresh branches.

2- You do not have time to monitor other's flaws and mistakes.

3- If Allah is with you, then who should you fear? If Allah is against you, then who should you implore?

4- The fire of envy eats the body, while excessive jealousy is an all-embracing fire.

5- If you are not prepared today, then you should know that you will not have time tomorrow.

6- Leave safely all gatherings of time-wasting and trivial arguments.

7- You can be, with your morals, even more beautiful than a garden.

8- Observe charity and you will be the happiest of people.

9- Do not concern yourself with Allah's creatures, for they are His matter. Ignore the envious and forget about the enemy.

10- Remember that the pleasure of what is prohibited is always followed by regret, remorse and punishment.

CHAPTER 2

⟨There is no might or power except with Allah ﷻ⟩.

1
A woman who defied the tyrant

W hen you look at the texts of Shari'ah in the Book of Allah (the Qur'an) and the Sunnah of His Prophet, you find that Allah ﷻ has praised the pious believing woman, saying:

⟨**Allah sets forth as an example to those who believe the wife of Pharaoh: Behold, she said: "O my Lord! Build for me in nearness to Thee a mansion in the Garden and save me from Pharaoh and his doings and save me from those that do wrong**⟩[1]

Think about how Allah ﷻ has made this woman (Asiyah ﷻ) a living example for the believing men and women, and a manifest sign for everyone who seeks to follow the guidance of Allah ﷻ in their life.

Asiya's request shows how sensible and rightly guided she was, as she asked to be near the Generous Lord and away from the evil, tyrant and disbeliever: her husband the Pharaoh. She refused to live in the palace of her husband, with all its servants and luxury, and preferred to be with in a lasting house near the Lord of the Worlds, in an Assembly of

---

[1] Surat at-Tahreem, Verse 11.

14

Truth in the presence of The Omnipotent Sovereign (Allah, the One, The Owner of Majesty and Honour).

She was a great woman, whose dignity and truthfulness led her to challenge her tyrant husband with the word of truth and faith, and so she was tortured for the Sake of Allah ﷻ, but she eventually earned a home in the company of her Lord, who has made her an example for every believing man and woman, until the Rising of the Hour.

> *"Be optimistic, even if you are in the eye of the storm."*

2
You have a fortune of blessings

My sister, there is relief along with every hardship, there is a smile after a tear, and there is day after night. The clouds of worry will dissolve, the night of anxiety will be lifted, and distress will end by the Will of Allah ﷻ.

You should know that you are rewarded by Allah ﷻ; if you are a mother, your children will be great supporters for Islam, when you bring them up on righteous education. They will supplicate for you in their prostration to Allah ﷻ and in their night prayers, before dawn.

It is a great blessing to be a loving and compassionate mother. It is a sufficient honour and pride for you that the mother of Muhammad ﷺ was a woman who offered a great leader to mankind, the generous Prophet Muhammad ﷺ.

It is in your ability to invite women to the Way of Allah ﷻ wisely with a good word and sound preaching; argue with them in the manner that is best and most gracious; setting a good example with your true guidance, as you follow the Right Path. In fact, a woman can achieve with her behaviour and righteous deeds that which cannot be achieved by means of sermons and lectures. How many a woman has lived in a particular area, and her neighbours started to talk about her good behaviour as a good Muslim woman, who observes her

Hijab, obeys her husband and is very kind to her neighbours. Her good conduct made her an excellent example for other people to follow.

"Tomorrow, the worries will go and solace will take place."

3
It is honourable enough for you that you are Muslim

Everything that happens to you for the Sake of Allah ﷻ is an expiation for your sins, by the Will of Allah ﷻ. Take the glad tidings in this Hadith: "When a woman observes the five times of prayer, fasts during Ramadan, preserves her chastity and obeys her husband, she may enter by any of the gates of Paradise she wishes." They are easy deeds for those who receive the Help of Allah ﷻ to achieve them. So perform these great obligations so that you meet the Merciful Lord who will make you happy both in this world and in the Hereafter.

Observe the Commands of Shari'ah and follow the teachings in the Qur'an and the Sunnah of the Prophet ﷺ, for you are a Muslim, and this is a great and sublime honour.

Many a woman was born in the lands of disbelief; they are either Christian, Jewish, communist or any other faith which opposes the religion of Islam; but you have been selected by Allah ﷻ to be a Muslim, among the followers of Prophet Muhammad ﷺ, and among the followers of 'Aishah, Khadijah and Fatimah, may Allah be pleased with them all.

Congratulations to you for observing your five daily prayers, fasting the month of Ramadan, performing the pilgrimage (Hajj), and observing the legal Hijab.

Congratulations to you if you are pleased with Allah ﷻ as your Lord, Islam as your religion and Muhammad ﷺ as your Prophet.

> *"Your gold is your religion, your jewellery your morals, and your wealth your ethics."*

4
A believing woman and a disbelieving one are not equal

It is easily possible for you to stay happy when you ponder on one fact: the real life of the Muslim woman in a Muslim country and the real life of the disbelieving woman in a country of unbelief.

The Muslim woman in the land of Islam is a woman who believes in Allah ﷻ and His Messenger ﷺ, gives charity, fasts the month of Ramadan, observes the Hijab, obeys her husband, fears her Lord, is kind to her neighbours and merciful towards her children; so congratulations to her for the great reward she receives for pleasing her Lord.

As for the disbelieving woman in the land of unbelief, she is indecent (uncovers herself to people), ignorant, foolish; she exposes herself offensively in fashion shows, as a cheap product; she easily loses her honour and dignity as she lacks faith.

Therefore, you can compare between these two images, only to find that you are the happiest and the most dignified, and praise to Allah ﷻ.

> *"All people will live, the owner of the palace and the owner of the hut, but who is the happier?"*

5

Laziness is the companion of failure

I advise you to remain in activity and not resign yourself to idleness. You should rise and refresh your house or home library, perform your tasks, pray and recite the Book of Allah, read other beneficial books, listen to an interesting lecture, sit with your neighbour and discuss with her anything that takes you both closer to Allah ﷻ. It is with such activities that you will taste happiness and bliss. Be careful not to surrender to idleness or inactivity, for it will make you inherit all sorts of worries and devilish whispers, which can only be removed by activity.

You have to take care of your looks, such as the beauty of your appearance inside your house. Conduct yourself well with your husband, children, relatives and friends; treat them well with the best smile and delightful welcome.

I warn you against all sorts of sins, for they are the reason of all sorrows, especially the sins which are common among women, such as the unlawful look, the uncovering (of the body) and sitting alone with foreign men; the cursing and slander of other people; the ungratefulness towards the right of the husband. Those sins are frequent among women, except the women who are blessed by Allah ﷻ. Therefore, be aware of the Anger of Allah ﷻ; it is by fearing Allah ﷻ

that you will guarantee happiness in this world and the Hereafter.

> *"When worries come up to you in numbers, say: la ilaha illa Allah (There is no god but Allah)."*

6
What you possess makes you above millions of women

Think about the whole world, does it not exist in hospitals with many patients lying on white beds, suffering from illness for many years? Are there not thousands of people in prisons behind bars, whose life is grim? Are there not in care houses and hospitals many people who have lost their minds and became mentally ill? Are there not many poor people who live in broken tents and huts and struggle to find their daily bread? Are there not many women who have lost their sight, or hearing or one of their limbs or even their minds, following a road accident, while you are safe, secure and in good health?

Therefore, you should praise Allah ﷻ for His Blessings. Do not spend your time in matters which do not please Allah ﷻ, such as sitting for long hours watching satellite channels, which mostly diffuse cheap, fake and facile programmes. These programs instil grief and sorrow in the heart and rend the body unable to perform its duties. Try, however, to select only the beneficial, such as a lecture or a debate, or an interesting medical programme, or some news of concern to Muslims.

Avoid watching all the superficial programmes and the impudence displayed on many TV channels, for they abandon decency and spread immorality.

"Leave the wrongdoer to the Supreme in the Hereafter, where there is no ruler but Allah ﷻ."

7
Build a palace in Paradise for yourself

Think about how many generations have passed away? Have they taken their wealth with them? Have they taken their palaces with them? Have they carried their social or professional status with them? Have they been buried with gold and silver? Have they moved to the other world in their private cars and jets?

No! They were even stripped of their own clothes and coverings and were entered inside their graves in their shroud. Then, every one of them is asked: Who is your Lord? Who is your prophet? What is your religion?

Therefore, you should prepare yourself for such day, and do not be annoyed about missing out on anything in this world, for it is cheap and momentary. Only your good deeds will earn you rewards. Allah ﷻ says:

{Whoever works righteousness man or woman and has faith verily to him will We give a new life that is good and pure and We will bestow on such their reward according to the best of their actions}[1]

> *"Illness is a message in which there are glad tidings, while good health is a precious jewel."*

---

[1] Surat an-Nahl, Verse 97.

{None has the right to be worshipped except You. How Perfect You are, verily I was among the wrong-doers}

8
Do not tear your heart with your own hands

Avoid any activity which wastes your time, such as reading obscene magazines, with naked pictures and depressing ideas, or atheistic books, or immoral world stories. Replace them with beneficial books and Islamic magazines, with articles to benefit you, both in this world and in the Hereafter.

There are some books and articles which induce doubt in one's mind and deviation in one's decisions. These are the traces of the corrupt culture which invaded our land from the polytheist world.

You should know that Allah ﷻ has the keys to the world of the Unseen. He ﷻ is the One who drives away grief and worries. You only have to invoke Him and constantly repeat the following supplication: "O Allah, I seek refuge in You from grief and sorrow, weakness and laziness, miserliness and cowardice, the burden of debts and from being overpowered by men."

When you repeat this supplication and reflect upon its meanings, Allah ﷻ will relieve you from all your worries, at His Will.

> *"Use all your time in planting righteous deeds."*

❨...Or who listens to the (soul) distressed
when it calls on Him❩

9
You are dealing with a Generous Lord

Feel the good tidings, for Allah ﷻ has prepared a great reward for you; He says: ❨**Their Lord responds to them: I will not let the deeds of any doer among you – male or female – go to waste❩**[1]

Allah ﷻ has promised women as He ﷻ has promised men; He ﷻ praised women as He ﷻ has praised men; He ﷻ says: ❨**Men who surrender unto Allah, and women who surrender, and men who believe and women who believe, and men who obey and women who obey, and men who speak the truth and women who speak the truth, and men who persevere (in righteousness) and women who persevere, and men who are humble and women who are humble, and men who give alms and women who give alms, and men who fast and women who fast, and men who guard their modesty and women who guard (their modesty), and men who remember Allah much and women who remember--Allah has prepared for them forgiveness and a vast reward❩**[2] and this proves that you are a sister and companion of man. Your reward is preserved with Allah ﷻ and you have plenty of righteous deeds to do in your house and society to guide you to the Pleasure of Allah ﷻ.

---

[1] Surat al-'Imran, Verse 195.
[2] Surat al-Ahzab, Verse 35.

Take Asiyah ﷺ, the wife of the Pharaoh, as your example to follow in your life, or Maryam ﷺ, or Khadijah, 'Aishah, Asma' and Fatimah ﷺ. They all headed the chosen, righteous, believing women, who observed their prayers and fast. Follow their footsteps and read their eminent biography and you will discover goodness and peace.

> *"Wipe away the tears of the orphan and you will gain the Pleasure of the All-Merciful and a residence in Paradise."*

10
You are the winner in any case

You have to be extremely patient in order to expect the rewards from Allah ﷻ.

If you are stricken by worry and sorrow, then you should know that it is but expiation of your sins.

If you happen to lose one of your children, then you should know that he will intercede for you with the One and only God, Allah ﷻ.

If you suffer from a bodily illness, then you are rewarded by Allah for being patient.

You will be rewarded for every trial you go through, be it hunger, illness, or poverty; provided you are patient, for Allah ﷻ preserves the trust for everyone until the Hereafter.

> *"Salat is a guarantee to delight one's mind and chase away worries."*

CHAPTER 3

{Take whatever I gave you and be among the thankful}

1
Count Allah's blessings upon you

When you get up in the morning, remember the state of thousands of wretched women while you are blessed, thousands of hungry women, while you are fed in full, thousands of detained women, while you are free, thousands of ill women, while you are safe and well.

Think about the many tears on women's cheeks, the many pains in a mother's heart, and the many cries in children's throats, while you are cheerful and pleased. Praise and thank Allah ﷻ for His Mercy and Generosity upon you.

Be truthful to yourself and count the blessings of everything you possess, such as money, beauty, children, residence, food, water, medicines and clean air.

Rejoice and be happy.

"With a penny, you can buy the supplication of the poor and the love of the destitute."

⟨Be pleased with what Allah ﷻ has apportioned for you, and you will be the richest of all people⟩

2
Contend with little to make you happy than plenty to make you sad

Your lifetime that is counted is that of happiness, delight, peace and contentment. Greed and voracity are not basically part of your life, because they oppose your good health and beauty.

Therefore, you should preserve your satisfaction with what Allah ﷻ has apportioned for you, your faith in destiny, and your optimism about the future.

Be likeable and nice like a butterfly, with a delightful look, which is less attached to things and flies from one rose to another and from one garden to another.

Or be like a bee, which eats only that which is good and produces only the good. When it falls upon a stem, it does not break it. It absorbs the essence of the flower and gives the best honey, without any biting. It flies with love and lands on the flowers with affection.

> *"Allah ﷻ loves the repentant, because they return to Him for help about their condition."*

3
Think of the heavens and do not think of the dust

Be a high-minded woman, with far-reaching aims. I call on you to be always ambitious, and beware of any breakdown or disintegration.

You should know that life is defined in minutes and seconds. Always try hard to be like an ant in seriousness, determination and steadfastness.

Always repent to Allah ﷻ. If you happen to commit a sin again, then return to Allah ﷻ in repentance. Try hard to memorise verses of the Qur'an; if you forget any of them, then go back to memorise them again.

It is very important that you do not feel failure and despair, because history does not recognize the term "despair", while the intellect does not acknowledge the bitter end. There should always be trial for rectification.

Indeed, lifetime is like a body; it is possible to submit it to an aesthetic surgical operation. Life is like a building, which can be refined or rebuilt anew; it can be adorned or newly decorated. So, beware of the school of failure and disappointment. Remove all bad expectations from your

mind, such as disasters, calamities or misfortunes, for Allah
ﷻ says:
❲**In Allah you should ever put your trust, if you are faithful**❳[1]

> *"Abstaining from a sin is jihad, while persisting in it is obstinacy."*

---

[1] Surat al-'Imran, Verse 122.

4

Rather a modest house with faith than a palace with oppression

A Muslim woman who lives in a hut, worshipping her Lord, praying her five daily prayers, and fasting the month of Ramadan is happier than a woman who lives in a lofty palace.

A woman who lives in a modest house, having wheat bread and bottled water as provision, and clinging to her copy of the Qur'an, is more happy than a woman who lives in a towering castle, while she does not know her Lord and does not follow His Prophet Muhammad ﷺ.

You should understand the real meaning of happiness. It is not the narrow context fancied by many people; that of wealth, furnishings, clothing, food, drinks, cars, etc.

Happiness is rather the pleasure of the heart, the peace of mind, the calmness of the soul, the happiness of the self, the delight of the heart, the righteousness of morals, good conduct, satisfaction and contentment.

"How can anyone who harms a Muslim or wrongs a servant of Allah ﷻ feel fine?"

⟨Put your trust in The Living (Allah ﷻ) who does not die⟩

5
Divide your time on the obligations

Try your luck with a beneficial book or an interesting audio-visual lecture. Listen to a good recitation of the Qur'an, in case that one particular verse might shake your mind and get deep into your soul to address your feelings and your heart. It will plant right-guidance and remove despair and doubt.

Read the books of the Sunnah and the traditions of the Prophet ﷺ in "Riyad as-Salihin" (the Garden of the Righteous) for example, to find the convenient medicine and beneficial knowledge to safeguard you from all kinds of deficiency and corruption.

Your remedy exists in the Revelation both in the Qur'an and the Sunnah; your tranquillity is your faith; your pleasure is in the prayer; the safety of your heart is in your submission to Allah's ﷻ commands; peace of mind is in your contentment with whatever is bestowed upon you; the beauty of your face is in your smile; the protection of your honour is in your observance of the Hijab, and the calmness of your mind is in the supplications.

> *"Beware of the supplication of the oppressed and the tears of the deprived."*

⟪In order that you may not despair over matters that pass you by or exult over favours bestowed upon you⟫

6
Our happiness is different from their happiness

Who told you that the distracting music, the rude songs, the destructive TV series, the outrageous play, the indecent magazine and the rude movie cause happiness and joyfulness?
Whoever said such statement has lied!

In fact, these means of entertainment are keys to misery; they lead to all sorts of worry, sorrow and anxiety. This was admitted by many people who have used such ways of entertainment and have now repented from them.

You should leave such miserable life; the life of those who deviated from the Right Path of Allah ﷻ.

Bring yourself to a humble recitation of the Qur'an, a beneficial reading, a spiritual advice, a brilliant lecture, a rewarding charity and a sincere repentance.

Come to spiritual gatherings and dedicated supplications, in the hope that Allah ﷻ accepts your repentance and fills your heart with peace and serenity.

> *"The sound heart is free of any kind of polytheism, cheating, hatred or envy."*

⟨O my Lord! Expand my breast for me.⟩

7
Go aboard the ship of salvation

I have read tens of stories of men and women artists, both the living and the dead, those who have led a distracting life, and I said to myself: Oh, what a pity! Where are the Muslim men and women, the believing men and women, the truthful men and women, the fasting men and women, the devout worshipping men and women?

Is this limited life expandable so that these people allow themselves to waste it in such irresponsible way, in the world of sin?

Do you possess another life other than this one?
Do you have covenant from Allah ﷻ that you will not die?
No, by Allah! These are but deceptive thoughts and fallacious hopes.

Put yourself into account for all your deeds, and then renew your course in life. Quicken your pace and get on board the ship of salvation.

> *"The wise woman turns the desert into a rich garden."*

8
A prostration to Allah ﷻ is a key to happiness

The first page of happiness in today's book and the first remedy card in the day's record is the dawn (fajr) prayer.

Start your day with the dawn prayer, so that you will be in Allah's Protection and Care.

Allah ﷻ will safeguard you from all evil and will guide you to all good. He ﷻ will deny any vice and will direct you to every virtue.

Allah ﷻ does not bless one's day which has not started with the dawn prayer.

The dawn prayer is the first sign of Allah's acceptance of one's deeds; it is the title of the book of success, the sign of victory, dignity and mastery.

Congratulations to everyone who performs and observes the dawn prayer, and misery to everyone who neglects it.

"Ineffective arguments and futile dispute drive away clarity and purity."

9
Lessons from great women of the past

Take as an example the old lady whose son was detained by the tyrant Al-Hajjaj, who swore by Allah to kill him. She showed a great deal of trust in Allah ﷻ and said with determination and courage: "Had you not killed him, he would have died (anyway)!"

Be like the Persian old lady in her reliance on Allah ﷻ, as when she was away from her chickens, raised her eyes to the sky and said: "O Allah, safeguard the home of my chickens, for you the Best of all protectors!"

Be steadfast like Asma' ◈, the daughter of Abu Bakr ◈, who when she saw her son, Abdullah ibn Al-Zubayr ◈, executed and crucified, uttered her famous words: "Has the time not come for this knight to walk!"

Be like Al-Khansa' who offered four sons as martyrs for the Path of Allah ﷻ; and said when she was informed of their deaths: "I praise Allah ﷻ for honouring me with their deaths as martyrs in His Path…"

Think about the glorious history of those women and learn from their glorified biography.

> *"Take from the breeze its tenderness, from al-misk its perfume, and from the mountain its firmness."*

⟨So do not lose heart nor fall into despair, for you must gain mastery if you are true in faith⟩

10
You are the most brilliant person in the universe

You are, with your beauty, more brilliant than the sun. You are, with your morals, more pure than musk. You are, with your humbleness, more elevated than the moon. So conserve your beauty with faith, your pleasure with contentment, and your chastity with the Hijab.

You should know that your jewellery is not gold, silver or diamonds, but rather the prayer you perform in the middle of the night, the thirst you feel in the midday heat when fasting the day for Allah ﷻ, the charity you give which is known only by Allah ﷻ, the tear of remorse which wipes away your sin, the long prostration to Allah on the mat of worship, and your modesty before Allah ﷻ when stirred by the devilish temptations of Satan.

Therefore, you should cover yourself with the raiment of righteousness, for you are the most beautiful woman in the world, even with torn garments. Wear the cover of decency, for you are the most brilliant woman in the universe, even with bare feet.

Be careful of the life of the unbelievers, the insolent, the shameless women, for they are the fuel of the Hellfire, which as Allah ﷻ says: ❨**Only the most wretched must endure**❩[1],

"In every place, you will find darkness in your life, so you only have to light up the lamp within yourself."

---

[1] Surat al-A'la, Verse 15.

CHAPTER 4

(When you wake up in the morning
do not wait for the evening)

1
O woman of high status

O truthful Muslim woman! O repentant believing woman! Be like a palm tree which is away from all evil; harmless tree; it is pelted with stones, yet it throws back dates. It is constantly green, both in summer and winter, and it is mostly beneficial.

Be highly minded above all trivial matters, safeguarded from all that violate decency.

Let your talk be remembrance of Allah ﷻ, your outlook be a precept, and your silence be your thinking. It is in this manner that you will discover happiness and rest.

Allah ﷻ will make you approved and welcomed by all people; you will receive their good praise and true supplications.

Allah ﷻ will drive away all clouds of anxiety, the phantom of fear, and the mountain of worry from you.

Sleep in the company of people's supplications for you, and rise up in their praise for you.

It is in this high status that you learn that happiness is not in the abundance of wealth, but rather in the obedience of the All-Praiseworthy, the Almighty Allah ﷻ.

> *"Do not despair of yourself, for the change is very slow, and you will face many obstacles to impede your determination; so do let them overpower you!"*

2

The second golden jewel: be grateful for Allah's blessings and use them well

U se the blessings of Allah ﷻ with gratefulness. Enjoy the blessing of water in your drinking, washing and ablution. Enjoy the blessing of the sun as light and heat. Enjoy the blessing of the moonlight as gratification of the eye. Enjoy picking fruits, crossing rivers, sailing the seas or travelling through desert lands and thank Allah, the Almighty, the All-Merciful.

Benefit from all these blessings, which Allah ﷻ has bestowed upon you, and do not ungrateful towards them. Do not be like those on whom Allah ﷻ says: ❲**They recognise the favours of Allah, and then they deny them.**❳[1]

Before looking for the flower's thorns, look at its beauty.
Before complaining about the heat of the sun, enjoy its light.
Before grumbling about the darkness of the night, remember its calmness and tranquillity.

Why do people have this dark pessimistic outlook about things?
Why do people change the blessings from their course?

---

[1] Surat an-Nahl, Verse 83.

Allah ﷻ says about them: ⟨**Have you not seen those who have changed the favour of Allah into blasphemy**⟩[1]

Take Allah's blessings, and accept them well at heart and praise Him for them.

> *"The transition from wrong to right is a long adventure, yet it is beautiful."*

---

[1] Surat Ibrahim, Verse 28.

3

The third golden jewel: There is ample provision along with constant istighfar (seeking Allah's Forgiveness)

A woman said: "My husband died while I was in my thirties, and I had with him five children. The whole world darkened in my eyes and I cried a lot until I was worried about my sight.

I cursed my luck and I despaired a lot as I was surrounded with worries; for my children were small and we did not have a sufficient income. I used to spend carefully from the rest of some money inherited from my late father.

One day, as I was sitting in my room, I turned the radio on the Holy Qur'an channel, and a sheikh said: "The Messenger of Allah ﷺ said: 'Whoever seeks Allah's Forgiveness incessantly, Allah ﷻ will relief him from his worries and release him from his troubles' so I started asking Allah ﷻ for forgiveness with persistence and ordered my children to do so continually.

By Allah, after only a period of six months, a new development project about some old properties of ours came up, and I was recompensed with millions.

Our life changed consequently. My son became the first among the students of our region; he memorised the Qur'an and was highly estimated by people around him.

Our home was filled with good and benefits and we enjoyed a peaceful life. Allah ﷻ reformed all my sons and daughters, and released me from all grief and worries, and I became the happiest woman."

"If you give in to despair, you will never learn anything or enjoy happiness ever!"

⟨Truly no one despairs of Allah's Mercy except those who have no faith⟩

4
Supplication cancels tribulation

The wife of a truthful, devout, righteous friend was stricken with cancer; she is the mother of his three children; so he became extremely depressed and the whole world darkened in his eyes.

One of the scholars recommended that he should perform the night prayers and supplicate in times before daybreak. He advised him to seek Allah's Forgiveness and recite the Qur'an over the water of zam-zam and offer it to his wife. He continued to do so until Allah ﷻ answered his prayers. He made his wife wash her body with the water of zam-zam after reciting the Qur'an over it, and used to sit with from the dawn prayer until the sunrise and from the sunset until the isha (evening) prayer.

They both used to invoke Allah's Forgiveness and Mercy persistently and submissively, until Allah ﷻ released her from pains and cured her disease. He ﷻ replaced her skin and hair with even more beautiful ones, as she became firmly attached to the night prayer.

O sister, if you become ill, flee to Allah ﷻ, and seek constantly His Forgiveness in your supplications. Expect the good tidings from Allah ﷻ, for He ﷻ answers the prayers of His truthful sincere slaves, and relieves them from all evil.

Allah ﷻ says: ﴾**Or who listens to the (soul) distressed when it calls on Him**﴿[1]

> *"Examine your past and your present, for life is made up of continuous tests, and one has to come out victorious through them."*

---

[1] Surat an-Naml, Verse 62.

5
Beware of despair and hopelessness

Ayoung man was put in prison and his mother lost her sleep, worrying about him, because he was her only child. She had been crying about his detention until she had no more tears left. So Allah ﷻ guided her to repeat the statement: "There is no might or power except with Allah". She kept on repeating this great statement, which is one of the treasures of Paradise, and so after a few days – after she despaired about the release of her son – she was surprised at her son knocking at her door. She was extremely delighted and filled with joy; such is the reward of anyone who supplicates to his Lord and refers her matters to Him ﷻ.

O sister, you have to observe the saying of this great word "There is no might or power except with Allah", for it is the secret of all happiness and salvation.

Keep it constantly on your tongue in order to chase away all sorts of worries, and give yourself the good tidings that relief from Allah ﷻ is close.

Beware not to break the link of hope and do not give in to despair, for there is always relief after hardship. This is the pattern of Allah ﷻ in this life, as decreed by Him.

Therefore, one should always have good thoughts about his Lord, rely on Him, ask Him for anything, and wait for the freedom from grief and sorrow from Him Alone.

> *"Do not let your worries and troubles be the subject of your talk, because, in doing so, you create a barrier between you and your happiness."*

6
Let your house be the kingdom of honour and love

Dear sister, observe staying in your house, except for an important matter, for your house is the secret of your happiness; Allah ﷻ says: ⟨**Stay in your houses**⟩[1].

When you stay in your house, you will discover the savour of happiness, and safeguard your honour and decency.

The marginal woman is the one who goes out shopping unnecessarily; her main concern is to visit the different shopping stores for the latest fashions, asking for any new or unusual clothes. She does not have a religious worry; she does not carry a message for others; she does not seek any knowledge. She is rather a free-spender in food and clothes...

I warn any Muslim sister against going out, except in necessity. Her house remains her place of happiness and security.

---

[1] Surat al-Ahzab, Verse 33.

Make your house a gathering of love and a source of a blessed gift.

> *"Do not confide your troubles except to those who help you with their counselling which brings forward happiness."*

7
Let your house be the kingdom of honour and love

Leave aside any involvement in futile arguments and debatable matters, because such debates lead to depression and dejection.

Do not always try to convince people in issues which bear many opinions. Try instead to lay down your point of view in a calm manner, without any firmness, and leave aside all sorts of argumentative and criticising answers, because they make you lose your peace of mind and present you in a repulsive image.

When you give your opinion in a calm and welcomed manner, you win people's hearts and their approval.

You should know that slander and backbiting draw all sorts of grief and regret; it deprives you of any reward and accumulates more sins upon you, and throws you in the world of unease.

Concern yourself in reforming your shortcomings instead of counting those of other people; for Allah ﷻ did not create us with perfect manners. We all rather have many defects and flaws.

> *"The mother whose child has fallen from a high position should not waste time in yelling and crying, she should rather rush to treat his injuries!"*

8

Have a shining spirit and the whole universe will cheer you

L ook at life in a more optimistic way, for it is a gift from Allah ﷻ to humanity.

Accept the gift of The One God (Allah ﷻ) and grab it with joyfulness and exuberance.

Welcome every morning with its daylight of beautiful sunlit beams.

Welcome every night with its calm and cool nature.

Breathe in the fresh air and smell the scent of roses while praising the Lord.

Think about the wonderful creation of the universe.

Benefit from all Allah's gifts and provisions on earth, such as the beauty of flowers, the fresh air, the fragrance of roses, the sun's heat and the moonlight.

Change these gifts and provisions into useful means for achieving your obedience to Allah ﷻ.

Praise and thank Allah ﷻ for His Blessing and Grace.

Beware not to be surrounded by nightmares of worries and grief which would prevent you from perceiving Allah's Grace.

You should know that Allah ﷻ has created all these blessings only to help us in our obedience to Him ﷻ, for He ﷻ says: ﴾**O you Messengers! Eat of the good thing and act rightly**﴿[1]

"The best of generosity comes from those who do not own anything, yet they know the value of the word and the smile; and how many people give as if they slap you in the face!"

---

[1] Surat al-Mu'minun, Verse 51.

9
No one has ever achieved complete happiness

You are wrong if you think that life should all go your way; this cannot be realised except in Paradise.

In this life, the matter is proportional; not all your wishes can be achieved. There will rather be some trial and tribulations, such as illnesses and misfortunes. Be grateful in days of ease and patient in days of hardship.

Do not live in a world of utopia, where you wish to be healthy without being ever sick, or wealthy without being poor, or happy without any worries, or you wish to have a husband without any defect, or a friend without any shortcoming. This can never take place in reality.

Be firm in avoiding all negative thinking and ignore other people's mistakes. Reflect upon the merits, advantages and good qualities.

You have to think good of Muslims, seek excuse for them and rely only upon Allah ﷻ; for people are not worth relying on; Allah ﷻ says: ⟨**They will be of no use to thee**⟩

> *"Do not accept to live with darkened spots in your life, for light is accessible and you only have to switch it on."*

⟨Whoever fears Allah, He will make matters easy for him.⟩[1]

10
Enter the Garden of Knowledge

Understanding Islam is one of the means of achieving happiness. Indeed, learning about Islam brings delight and pleases the Lord. The Prophet ﷺ said: "When Allah ﷻ intends good for a person, He grants him understanding of the religion."

So, read available beneficial books which will increase your knowledge and understanding of Islam, such as "Riyad as-Salihin", "Fiqh as-Sunnah", "Fiqh ad-Dalil", easy books of "Tafsir" (Interpretations of meaning of the Qur'an), and any useful essays.

Remember that the best of your deeds is to know what Allah ﷻ meant in His Book (the Qur'an) and what the Prophet ﷺ intended to convey in his Sunnah.

Study frequently the Qur'an with your sisters; memorize whatever you can of it; listen to its recitation and act upon it, because ignorance of Islam draws grief and distress in the heart.

---

[1] Surat at-Talaq, Verse 4.

Get a home library, even a small one, with valuable and useful books and tapes. Beware of wasting time listening to songs or watching TV soaps, for you will be accounted for every second of your life; so use your time in pleasing Allah, the Exalted, Almighty.

> *"The hardest of all hardships could be made easier by the smile of confident person."*

CHAPTER 5

《... it may be that Allah will afterwards create a new situation to develop》[1]

1
Remember the shed tears and the broken hearts

A writer said: If you believe that you have taken a covenant with time that all your affairs will go your way and that you will be granted only what you desire, then it is appropriate to let yourself grieve freely every time you miss out on something.

However, if you believe in the ethical standard of time in its acceptance and refusal, its giving and its denial, and that it does not offer you something without coming to get it back, and that this is the way in the life of all the sons of Adam, whether they live in palaces or huts, then you should reduce your grief and wipe away your tears. In fact, you are not the first person to be stricken with the arrow of time (misfortune), and your problems are nothing new in the archives of grief and calamities.

> *"Stop regretting your sin and think about the good virtue with which you are going to replace it"*

---

[1] Surat at-Talaq, Verse 1.

2
These people are not happy

Do not look at people who live in lavishness and extravagance, for their real world deserve pity not envy.

There are people whose main concern is to spend lavishly upon themselves and spare no effort in satisfying their whims and low desires – whether permissible or forbidden – and such people are never happy. They are rather living a hard life of worry and grief, because whoever deviates from the Way of Allah 🕮 and disobeys Him will never experience real happiness.

Do not believe that people who live in luxury are happy and delighted, not at all!

There are poor women who live in mud huts yet happier than those who sleep on feather beds and silky sheets in lofty palaces; because the poor, devout believing woman is in a better condition than the one who has gone astray from the Way of Allah 🕮.

> *"Happiness exists in you, so you should focus your efforts on yourself."*

3
The Way of Allah is the best of all ways

What is happiness? Does happiness exists in money or status or lineage? There are many answers... but let us check the happiness of this woman:

A man had an argument with his wife, so he said to her: "I am going to make you miserable." She calmly replied: "You cannot." He said to her: "Why not?" so she replied: "Had happiness been in money, you would have deprived me from it, or in my jewellery, you would have denied them to me, but it (happiness) is not something neither you nor other people possess. I find my happiness in my faith, and my faith is located in my heart, and no one has any control over my heart except my Lord, Allah 🕮."

This is the true happiness; happiness of the faith. No one feels it except those whom their heart, soul and mind are filled with the love of Allah. The one who truly has control over happiness is the One True God; so seek happiness from Him by obeying Him 🕮.

The only way to find happiness is by learning about Islam, the true religion, which is the Message of the Messenger of Allah, Muhammad 🕮.

---

[1] Surat Muhammad, Verse 19.

Whoever experiences this way will not mind if he sleeps in a mud hut or by the side of the road; he will be content with a piece of bread and he will be the happiest person in the world. But whoever strays from this way, he will experience a life of grief and disappointment.

> *"We need money to make a living, but it does not mean that we should live for the sake of money."*

4
When your grief becomes unbearable, seek help from Allah ﷻ.

Ibn al-Jawzi said: "A distressful matter made me so anxious that I felt constantly restless and worried, so I started to think deeply about the way to free myself from these worries by any means, but I could not find a way out. Then I came across this Verse:

❮**Whoever fears Allah, He will give him a way out**❯, and I knew that fearing Allah ﷻ and keeping one's duty to Him ﷻ is the only way out of any worry and distress. I resolved then to establish taqwa (being mindful of Allah ﷻ) and I found the way out."

I say reasonable people define piety as the way to everything good, for a misfortune takes place only as a result of a sin, and it can only be lifted by repentance. Distress, sadness and worry are punishments for committing sins, such as falling short in your prayers, or backbiting Muslim women, or not observing well the Hijab, or committing forbidden deeds.

Whoever violates the Way of Allah ﷻ will certainly pay for his carelessness. The One Who created happiness is the Most Gracious, the Most Merciful; so how can happiness be sought from anyone other than Him? If people had control over happiness, there would be no deprived, or sad or grieving person left on Earth.

"Chase away any despairing thought from your mind, focus on success and you will never fail."

5
Make everyday a new beginning

Keeping oneself away from the Way of Allah ﷻ draws only bitterness in life. All the potentials of intellect, strength, beauty and knowledge turn into calamities and misfortunes when it is kept away from the guidance of Allah and deprived from His blessings. It is for this reason that Allah ﷻ has warned people against ignoring His Commands.

As you walk on the road, a car comes at a high speed towards you and you feel that it will definitely hit you if you stay there. You then decide to move quickly away to save your life. Allah ﷻ wants to make His servants feel the same way when they face such calamities in the course of their life when they stay away from His Guidance. He ﷻ invites them to seek salvation with Him, Alone, as He ﷻ says:

⟨So flee to Allah. Verily, I am a plain warner to you from Him, and do not associate - in worship – any other god with Him. Verily, I am a plain warner to you from Him.⟩[1]

It is a return which requires from man to renew and reorganize his way of life; he should restart a new

---

[1] Surat Adh-Dhariyat, verse 50-51.

relationship with his Lord, based on righteous deeds and a covenant as expressed in the following supplication:

"O Allah, You are my Lord and there is no god but You. You created me and I am Your slave. I am trying my best to keep my oath (of faith) to You and to live in the hope of Your Promise. I seek refuge in You from the evil in what I have done. I acknowledge Your blessings upon me and I acknowledge my sins. So forgive me, for there is no one to forgive sins but You."

> *"If you fail in any of your deeds, you should not surrender to despair; do not worry and do not doubt that you will find a solution."*

The Prophet ﷺ said: "Your smiling at your Muslim sister is charity."

6
Women are like stars in the darkness of the skies

The righteous Muslim woman is the one who is kindly dutiful to her husband and obeys her Lord.

The Prophet ﷺ has praised this woman and considered her as the ideal woman for men to look for. When he ﷺ was asked which woman is best, he ﷺ answered: "The one who makes her husband happy when he looks at her; who obeys him when he orders her to do something; and who do not oppose him in a manner that he dislikes with regard to herself or his wealth."

When Allah ﷻ revealed the Verse: ❴**... and those who hoard up gold and silver**❵[1], 'Umar ibn Al-Khattab ﷺ went out followed by Thanban ﷺ until they reached the Prophet ﷺ, and 'Umar said: "O Prophet of Allah, this Verse has caused worry to your Companions." The Prophet ﷺ said: "Shall I inform you of something better for men to treasure? A righteous woman who pleases him when he looks at her; when he orders her to do something, she obeys him; and if he is away from her, she is faithful to him."

---

[1] Surat at-Tawbah, Verse 34.

The Messenger of Allah ﷺ has linked the admission of a woman into Paradise with her obedience to her husband. Umm Salamah, may Allah be pleased with her, said: "The Messenger of Allah ﷺ said: 'Any woman who dies when her husband is pleased with her will enter Paradise." So be such woman and you will enjoy real happiness.

> *"There is a place for you in the first row, as long as you add perfection to everything you do."*

7
Rather die than commit forbidden deeds

bdullah ibn 'Umar ibn Al-Khattab ﷺ reported a story about three people who stayed overnight in a cave, when a rock slipped down and blocked their exit. So they invoked Allah ﷻ to save them by relating their past righteous deeds.

The second of them said: "O Allah, I had a female cousin whom among all people I loved most – In another narration, he said: I used to love as much as any man can love a woman – I attempted to seduce her but she refused my advances, until when she became so poor, she came to me and I gave her a hundred and twenty dinars, on condition that she let me have my way with her. But when I sat between her legs, she said: "Fear Allah, and do not do it except in a lawful way."

This woman was pious. She initially rejected his sexual advances, but when she was so poor and desperate, she was forced into accepting his request; yet she reminded him of Allah ﷻ, and stirred his feelings of faith. She suggested that if he really wanted her, he should have the lawful way, by marrying her, and not committing adultery with her. Her words prompted him to abandon his sexual demands and he repented to Allah ﷻ.

By relating the story of how he did not commit adultery out of fear of Allah, he asked Allah ﷻ to help him and his friends in their ordeal, and so the rock moved slightly away on the day it blocked the exit of their cave.

"Learn how to co-exist with fear and it will vanish."

8
Verses to inspire

Allah ﷻ says:
《Allah will grant ease after hardship》[1]

《O you who believe, be patient, be supreme in steadfastness, be firmly stationed in the battlefield and fear Allah, that you may be successful》[2]

《... but give glad tidings to the patient, who when afflicted with calamity, say: "truly, to Allah, we belong, and truly to Him we shall return》[3]

《It is He Who sends down the rain after they have despaired, and spreads His Mercy》[4]

《Verily the steadfast will be paid their wages without stint》[5]

《There is no God but You. Glorified and Exalted be You! I have been of the wrongdoers》[6]

---

[1] Surat at-Talaq, Verse 7.
[2] Surat al-'Imran, Verse 200.
[3] Surat al-Baqarah, Verse 155-156.
[4] Surat Ash-Shura, Verse 28.
[5] Surat az-Zumar, Verse 10.
[6] Surat al-Anbiya', Verse 87.

The Qur'an calls on you to be happy, feel composed and trust your Lord. The Qur'an calls on you to open your heart to embrace the true promise of Allah, for He ﷻ did not create mankind to torment them, but rather to test them, purify them and discipline them.

Allah ﷻ is more merciful to man than the latter is to his mother or father.

Seek mercy, comfort and pleasure from Allah ﷻ, by remembering Him, being grateful to Him, reciting His Book, and following the Sunnah of His Messenger, Muhammad ﷺ.

> *"Prepare for the worst, and you will feel improvement in your conditions."*

"It is sufficient honour for women that the mother of Muhammad ﷺ was a woman."

9

Knowledge of the Most Merciful clears all grief

Allah ﷻ is the Most Generous and the Most Kind; He ﷻ provides for His slaves more than he hopes for before he even asks Him. He ﷻ appreciates little deeds and lets them prosper. He ﷻ forgives many misdeeds and wipes them away. Everyone in the Heavens and on the Earth asks Him and He is always engaged in some affairs. He ﷻ is not distracted by anything and He listens to everything. He ﷻ is not confused when asked about many things. He ﷻ is not annoyed by the persisting requests of people. He rather loves them when they persist on calling upon Him. He ﷻ gets angry when He is not asked. He ﷻ is kind to His slave when His slave does not care about Him. He ﷻ conceals His slave when His slave does not conceal himself. He ﷻ shows mercy to His slave when His slave does not show mercy to himself.

How could people's hearts not love Him when none guide to good deeds but Him?

He ﷻ is the One Who annuls sins, answers prayers, forgives mistakes, conceals that which ought to be concealed, relieves distress, helps the desperate, and grants blessings.

Allah ﷻ is the Most Bountiful of those who give, Most Merciful of those who show mercy, Most Generous of those sought for provision, Most Dominant of those sought for help, Most Sufficient of those relied on.

He ﷻ is more Merciful to His slave than a mother to her child, and He ﷻ rejoices more at the repentance of His slave than one who lost his camel, carrying his food and drink in a deserted land, and lost hope of finding it, then he finds it.

> *"Let your decision in your attempt to achieve happiness be a happy experience in itself."*

{Allah has set forth an example for those who believe: the wife of Pharaoh...}[1]

10
The blessed day

When you pray salat al-Fajr (the Dawn prayer), try to sit in a more humble manner; face the qiblah for ten or fifteen minutes, remember Allah ﷻ a great deal and supplicate Him.

Ask Allah ﷻ for a good day, a blessed day, a happy day, a successful day with no misfortunes, crises or problems.

Ask Allah ﷻ for a day with abundant provisions and goods, a day with no grief or distress.

It is from Allah ﷻ that we ask for happiness, provision and blessings.

It is such dedicated sitting which – by the Will of Allah – guarantees your preparation for such a good, blessed and beneficial day.

I recommend that whenever you have some work to do or are simply sitting to use such time in listening to the Qur'an from a tape or radio. Listen humbly to a recitation of some

---

[1] Surat at-Tahreem, Verse 11.

verses of the Qur'an from a devout reader who has a fine voice, which will cleanse your heart from any worry and grief, and so you will be in a better state than before.

> *"Do not worry about things that you are unable to carry out. Instead, spend your time in improving what you can do."*

CHAPTER 6

⟨... Yes! Certainly, the Help of Allah is near!⟩[1]

1
A sensible woman is the foundation of life happiness

A woman should offer a good welcome to her husband when he comes home. She should not be annoyed when she finds him tired or stressed. Rather, she should rush to meet his demands whatever they are, as soon as he enters the house, without asking him about the reasons of his stress or weariness.

Once he has changed his clothes, in which he went out, and settled down, he will most likely let her know about the reasons of his stress. If he does not, then there is no harm asking him, provided she does it in a manner to make him feel that she is very much concerned and worried about the state in which he came home.

Should she feel able to help her husband overcome the cause of his worry, then she should not hesitate in doing so; for she will take the burden off her husband's mind, the fact which will make him feel that there is a precious person in his

---

[1] Surat al-Baqarah, Verse 214.

house, one that is more precious than all the jewels in the world...

> *"Do not feel miserable because you have not completed a particular work. You should know that the work of significant people is never concluded."*

2
Focus well on today only

One of the happiest people once said: "The beautiful day is the one in which we are in control of our affairs and not the opposite. It is the day when we control our desires and we do not submit to them. I can remember some of these days and will never forget them.

I consider a day to be the most beautiful day when on that day I took control of myself and managed to overcome the test of doubt about what I am able and unable to do.

A beautiful day is that on which I hesitated whether to carry out a deed which would attract people's praise or a deed which was not known to anybody. So I gave up people's praise and was pleased to carry out a deed which I would remember all my life, but no one has ever heard of.

A beautiful day is that on which I was about to be wealthy but would lose my dignity, so I preferred rather to be penniless than empty-minded.

These days are beautiful, and the most beautiful thing about them is that my worldly gain by them is very small, except if the gain is my perception of honouring myself about what I have done, then, with praise to Allah ﷻ, it is definitely great."

> *"Be happy with what you own, content with whatever Allah ﷻ has decreed for you, and give up all daydreams which do match your efforts and abilities."*

3
Give up the feeling that you are persecuted

This is a great rule which helps overcome anxiety and leads to success in life in a general way. It helps preserve friendship and happiness among the family, because a high-minded person perceives well people's nature, considers all changes, puts himself in other people's place and assesses both the hidden and obvious situations.

When it comes to anxiety, a high-minded person understands well realities, and knows, when faced with a problem or when he does not achieve what he wants, that this is the nature of life and that no one has it his way. Man may dislike something in which there is good for him, and may like something in which there is evil for him, but all the good is that which is decreed by Allah ﷻ.

A high-minded person feels that he is part of this vast universe, and accepts the fact that he has his share of pain, grief and also happiness. Therefore, he is not mentally distressed or painfully affected by any affliction. He does not suffer from any feeling of persecution which is felt by the one with little insight, who feels that he is the only one stricken by such problem, or that people are victimising him, or that he always has bad luck.

---

[1] Surat al-Ma'idah, Verse 95.

A high-minded person does not feel such feelings. Rather, he understands well the nature of life, and that he is part of it; therefore, he is content with it, as he endeavours to achieve the best in his life.

"Enjoy happiness now and do not wait until tomorrow."

4
How sweet is success after hardship

A successful person said: "I was born in a poor family, and I have experienced the bitterness of asking my mother for a piece of bread, while she did not have anything to give, not even a piece of a dry crust.

I left home at the age of ten, and got a job at the age of eleven. I used to study only a month every year. After eleven years of hard work, I had an ox and six sheep, which earned me eighty-four dollars. I never spent a penny in my life on my pleasures. I rather used to save every penny I earned from the day I grew up until I reached twenty-one.

I have experienced real tiredness and travelled miles away, asking people for a job to earn my living. When I reached the age of twenty-one, I went to the forests to collect wood, driving a farm cart carried by two oxen. I used to get everyday before dawn and would continue my hard work until after sunset, so that I earn six dollars at the end of the month.

Every one of those six dollars appeared to me like the moon on a dark night."

> *"If you have committed mistakes in the past, learn from them, and then forget about them, after you have taken a lesson from them.*

*⟨Say: "It is Allah that delivers you from these and all
(other) distresses⟩*

5
You will certainly adapt with your situation

I know a man whose foot was amputated in a surgery, so I
went to comfort him. He was a wise man of knowledge,
and I decided to tell him: "The nation does not expect
you to be a great athlete, or a champion wrestler. Rather, it
expects you to be a man with right opinions and good
thoughts, and you still possess such good qualities, praise to
Allah ﷻ.
When I visited him, he said to me:

"Praise to Allah ﷻ, my foot has accompanied me in a good
way for decades, and comfort lies in the soundness of one's
religion."

A wise man said:

"Peace of mind can be attained only with the acceptance of
the worst that can ever happen in life. This is due, from a
psychological perspective, to the fact that submissive
acceptance releases one's energy from its chains..." then he
added: "Still, there are thousands of people who are ready to
destroy their lives as a result of their anger, because they
refuse to accept their bitter real world; they refuse to save
whatever can be saved. Instead of trying to build up their
hopes once again, they indulge in a bitter fight with the past,

and surrender to anguish and grief, which leads to no solution at all.

Regretting a failed past or weeping strenuously over all the pains and losses that took place in it are signs of disbelief in Allah ﷻ and a displeasure of His Decree, according to Islamic judgment.

> *"Frustration is your arch enemy; it has the ability to destroy your peace of mind."*

6
Sound advice from a wise woman

There is a comprehensive advice which is among the best of all narrated advices of Arab women. It is the advice of Umamah ibn Al-Harith to her daughter, Umm Ilyas, daughter of 'Awf, on the night of her wedding. In her advice, she said:

"O my daughter, you are about to leave the place of which you have come out and made your first steps. Should a woman not a husband because of the wealth of her parents and their utmost need for her, you would have been the first of all people who do not need him; but women are created for men and men are created for women.

My advice is as follow: Submit to him with self-conviction; listen to him and obey him in matters which please Allah ﷻ.

Be mindful of what he sees and smells in you. Make sure that he does not see anything ugly in you and smells only pleasant fragrance from you.

Look out for the times of his meals and sleep. Do not let him feel hungry and do not disturb his sleep.

---

¹ Surat al-Baqarah, Verse 143.

Safeguard his property and watch over his children and servants. Your care means that you appreciate everything from him.

Do not disobey him in any matter, and do not reveal his secrets; for if you disobey him and disclose his secrets, you will earn his anger and hatred.

Do not express your joy when you see him sad, or show your sorrow when he is happy!"

> *"Your happiness does not depend on other people; it is in your hands."*

7
A woman accepted Allah's Judgment to please Him

Have you heard the case of the Juhani woman who committed adultery, then she remembered Allah 🕮 and repented to Him. She came to the Messenger of Allah, Muhammad 🕮, while she was pregnant, and asked him to apply the Punishment of Allah 🕮 on her; that is stoning her to death in order to purify her of her sin. She said: O Messenger of Allah, I have done something for which prescribed punishment must be imposed upon me, so impose that." The Prophet 🕮 called her master and said: "Treat her well, and when she gives birth, bring her to me." He did accordingly. Then the Prophet 🕮 pronounced judgment on her. Her clothes were tied around her and then he gave the order and she was stoned to death. He 🕮 then prayed over her dead body. Thereupon Umar 🕮 said to him: "O Messenger of Allah, you offer prayer for her although she had committed adultery!" The Prophet 🕮 replied: "She has made such repentance that if it were to be divided among seventy men of Medina, it would be enough. Have you found any repentance better than that she sacrificed her life for Allah, the Majestic?"

It was the impetus of faith which had driven her to seek purification, and prefer the Hereafter over this worldly life. Had she not had a strong faith, she would not have preferred

89

to be stoned to death (than facing her Lord on the Day of Judgment with a heavy sin like adultery).

Someone might say: "But why did she commit adultery, a misdeed which is committed only by people with weaker faith?"

The answer is: A person can be weak and may commit an unlawful act, because he is created from weakness. He might go astray because he is not perfect. He is likely to commit a mistake because he is created of haste. But when the seed of faith grows in his heart to become a lofty blooming tree, it will show his authentic origin and firm conviction.

This is what made this woman rush to the Messenger of Allah ﷺ, asking him to impose Allah's Punishment on her to purify her soul, seeking only Allah's Pleasure, Mercy and Forgiveness.

"Avoid being a constant complainer or an amateur one!"

8
She was mindful of Allah ﷻ and so Allah protected her

It was reported that a beautiful and rich woman was late to escape her house with her servants during the battle of Alexandria (Egypt); so the invading crusading army went inside her waving their swords, and one of them said to her: "Where is the money?"

She was terrified and answered: "The money is in these boxes inside the house" pointing to the sitting room where she stays. One of them said: "Do not be scared, for you will be with me, and you will enjoy all my wealth and kind company." She understood that he liked her and wanted her for himself, so she leaned towards him and said softly: "I want to use the bathroom." He thought that she had desired him, so he waved for her to go to relieve herself. When she left the room, the soldiers continued to search the room for the boxes. She then went out from the house door and entered a storage place filled with straw, and dug a hole where she hid herself covered with straw.

The soldiers started looking for her when they finished their looting, but they could not find her. So they took away the boxes and left.

The woman saved herself from capture by her cunning trick. Her servants had escaped being detained when they climbed the roof of the building.

The woman then said: "Safety of one's religion and honour is worth a lot more than the wealth which is kept by dignified people only for a purpose like this, because being poor is better than being detained and compelled to change one's religion."

Accept the inevitable truth, which is that you will encounter in your life things that you cannot change, yet you can deal with them through patience and faith."

9

The water of repentance is the purest

Allah ﷻ loves those who repent and those who purify themselves. His happiness about the repentance of His slave is greater than that of a man who when he lost his camel which carried his food and drink in the desert, he despaired and lied down by a tree waiting for death, but when he got up, he find his camel by his side, with his food and drink. So he grabbed and shouted with extreme happiness: "O Allah, You are my slave and I am Your Lord!"

Glory be to Allah, how Great and Merciful He is! He ﷻ is Happy with the repentance of His slave, who will win entry to His Paradise and earn His Pleasure.

He ﷻ calls on His believing slaves to repent, saying:

❨Turn to Allah in repentance, O believers, that you may be successful.❩[1]

Repentance requires cleaning the heart with one's tears and the torment of remorse. It is a burning in the heart and a grief in the mind; it is a breakdown in the soul and a tear in the eye. It is the beginning of the road to repentance, a

---

[1] Surat an-Nur, Verse 31.

capital of those who are successful, the first step of those answering the call of Allah ﷻ, and the key to righteousness.

The Muslim penitent invokes Allah's Mercy and Forgiveness, weeping and crying. When other people are relaxed, he is not; when others are calm and careless, his fear never ceased, as he stands before Allah ﷻ, with a grieving heart and a bowing head, remembering his greatest sins. His heart burns in the flames of remorse and his tears are overflowing. He frees himself of any onerous loads so that he gets ready for a swift crossing over the bridge of Hell on the Day of Judgment.

"Think positively, for when things get bad one day, it is merely a sign that another day filled with joy and happiness is on the horizon."

Allah ﷻ says about righteous women: ⟨They guard in their husband's absence what Allah has ordered them to guard⟩[1]

10
The first woman freedom fighter

She lived a life of luxury in the greatest and finest palace during her lifetime, with many male and female servants at her service. It was Asiyah, daughter of Muzahim, may Allah be pleased with her, the wife of Pharaoh. She was a woman with a weak body, yet safe and serene in her palace. The light of faith shone in her heart, so she defied her world of disbelief, which was ruled by her husband.

She had a transcending outlook, which went beyond the palace and its luxurious life. It is for this reason that she deserved to be remembered by the Lord, to present her as an example for those who believe, as He ﷻ says:

⟨Allah has set forth an example for those who believe, the wife of Pharaoh, when she said: "My: Lord, build for me a home with You in Paradise and save me from Pharaoh and his work, and save me from the people who are transgressors⟩[2]

The scholars said in their interpretation of this Verse: "Asiyah had chosen the neighbour before choosing the house. She deserved to be mentioned by the Prophet ﷺ

---

[1] Surat an-Nisa', Verse 34.
[2] Surat at-Tahreem, Verse 11.

among the women the accomplished women, when he ﷺ said: "Many men attained perfection, but no man did except Asiyah, the wife of Pharaoh and Maryam, daughter of 'Imran, may Allah be pleased with them. The merit of 'Aishah on women is like the superiority of tharid (a dish made of bread, meat and broth) over the rest of food."

This was the example of Asiyah, the believer, the lamp which lit in the darkness of Pharaoh's palace.

Is there a person who can light a lamp of faith for us, with a great example of patience and firmness upon the Message of Allah ﷺ?

> *"Control your thoughts and you will enjoy happiness"*

CHAPTER 7

⟨Verily, the Mercy of Allah is ever near to the good-doers.⟩[1]

1
Put your trust in your Lord and sleep well

I say to every woman who went to sleep, satisfied with her Lord's Pleasure and Decree, undeterred by the hurricane surrounding her, while sorrow never finds its way into her heart, and tears never settled in her eyes,

I say to every woman who lost children, parents, relatives and loved ones,

I say to every anxious and worried Muslim person,

May Allah magnify your reward and lift your rank.

Allah ﷻ says:

⟨Seek help through patience and Salah, and truly it is extremely heavy and hard except for Al-Khashi'in (those who obey Allah with submission)⟩[2]

'Ali ibn Abi Talib ﷺ said: "Patience in faith is like the head in the body."

Therefore, rejoice with the reward in the Hereafter, a place in Al-Firdous (the Garden), in the company of the One God

---

[1] Surat al-A'raf, Verse 56.
[2] Surat surat al-Baqarah, Verse 45.

(Allah ﷻ), as a compensation for all the efforts you have given.

Congratulations for your faith, patience and anticipation for rewards. You will know that you are the winner in any case; Allah ﷻ says: ❨**Give glad tidings to the patient**❩[1]

> *"Your self-confidence means finding a purpose for your life regardless of your age, and gaining more experience in this life."*

---

[1] Surat al-Baqarah, Verse 155.

2
Real blindness is that of the heart

There was a blind man who lived happily with a loving and faithful wife, a dutiful son and a loyal friend; but the only thing that spoiled his happiness was darkness in which he lived. He wished that he could see the light in order to witness his happiness with his own eyes.

An excellent doctor came to the village, so the blind man went and asked for a medicine to restore his eyesight. The doctor gave him eye-drops, instructed him to apply them regularly, and said to him: "In doing so, you may regain your eyesight at any moment."

The blind man continued using the eye-drops, despite the despair of people around him. But after using them for a few days, he was surprised to see the light. One day as he sat in his garden he was extremely happy and overjoyed, so he went inside the house to inform his loving wife, but he saw her in his room, betraying him with his friend. He could not believe what he saw, so he went to the next room and found his son stealing from his closet.

The blind man went out screaming: "This is not a doctor; this is a cursed sorcerer!"

---

[1] Surat Ash-Shura, Verse 19.

So he took a pin and pierced his eyes, to return to his happiness with which he was in harmony.

"Mental anxiety is more lethal than physical illnesses."

⟨Nay, verily, there is my Lord with me; He will guide me.⟩[1]

3
Do not set up a court for revenge, as you may be the first victim

Some people are too kind; they are not interested about taking their right in full. They overlook many things following their easy-going nature. They do not look comparatively into things or read between lines. Generally, they do not care about such things.

Other people are not tolerant and do not forget about their rights, even the size of a seed. They strive in every matter to gain their rights – and sometimes the right of others - and they are rarely pleased or satisfied with what they get.

It is natural that the kind and tolerant person is the one closer to peace of mind and away from anxiety. He is also near people's hearts and worthy of their love. The doors open in his way more than those who are in constant war with other people and who analyse all words and expressions, searching for evil intentions. Such persons bring worry to themselves in every way. They are disliked by people, who try to avoid them and close all doors of success in their face..

---

[1] Surat Ash-Shu'ara, Verse 62.

101

The Prophet ﷺ said: "May Allah ﷻ have mercy on a person who is tolerant when he sells, tolerant when he buys, and tolerant when he reclaims his dues from other people."

"Work for the present day and do not worry about what will come tomorrow"

⟨We have not sent down the Qur'an upon you to cause you distress⟩[1]

4
Distinction is the result of one's achievement

A rich man said: "I have no special feeling about being the richest man in the world. I live a normal life in a modest flat with my wife. I neither drink nor smoke and I do not like the billionaire's lifestyle, whose pictures filled the newspapers, with their luxury yachts, countryside mansions, wild parties and weddings to the most beautiful girls, which usually end in costly divorces worth millions of dollars.

I love my work and I am pleased with it. I usually take my own lunch with me to have in my office, and I do not feel extremely happy when I think about all the billions I own.

However, I feel delighted when I remember the fact that I have helped change my hometown (Tokyo) with its modest streets into a capital city to become the focal point of the world with its modern buildings, which I have introduced.

In brief, my happiness comes from my achievements.

"Regret cannot recover a ship from the bottom of the sea."

---

[1] Surat Ta-Ha, Verse 2.

103

5

The world of disbelief suffers from misery

Doctor Harold C Habein of The Mayo Clinic, gave a lecture to the American Association of Doctors and Surgeons, who work in industrial institutions, saying that he had studied a hundred and seventy two cases of businessmen, with an average age of forty four, and discovered that more than one third were suffering from one of three diseases, which are the result of stress, such as: heart problem, stomach ulcer and high blood pressure; and that before reaching the age of forty five!

Can a man who buys his success with a stomach ulcer or a heart problem call himself successful?

What benefit can he gain if he owns the whole world and loses his health? If a man owns the whole world, he would still sleep in one bed and eat three meals a day. So what is the difference between him and the employee who works in the field? Perhaps, the worker enjoys a deep sleep and tastes his meals better than the businessman with high status and rank.

Another distinguished physician, Doctor Alvarez said: "It has become clear that four out of five patients do not suffer from a physical illness. Rather, the cause of their illness is

---

[1] Surat az-Zumar, Verse 36.

fear, anxiety, hatred, selfishness, and the inability to create harmony between oneself and life."

"We neither possess the means to change the past nor draw a picture for the future as we want, so why do we kill ourselves out of regret about something which we cannot change?"

6
One of the morals of a life-partner

The good believing woman does not annoy her husband with too many demands. She is satisfied with what Allah ﷻ has decreed for her, and her example is in the family of the Prophet ﷺ.

'Urwah ؓ reported that his aunt 'Aishah, may Allah be pleased with her, used to say: "By Allah, O son of my sister, we used to watch the new moon come, then the following one, then the following one; three new moons in two months, and no fires were lit in the houses of the Messenger of Allah ﷺ."

I said: "O Aunt, what did you live on?" She replied: "The two black items: dates and water. But the Prophet ﷺ had some neighbours among the Ansar[1]; that had goats, so they used to send some of their milk to the Messenger of Allah ﷺ and we all drunk from it."

> *"The value of life is when a man lives every minute of it."*

---

[1] Muslims in Madinah who supported the Prophet ﷺ and his immigrant companions who came from Makkah.

7

Be content with what Allah ﷻ has decreed for you

How great was the statement of Hajar, may Allah be pleased with her – the wife of Prophet Ibrahim, may Allah have peace upon him, and the mother of Prophet Ismail, may Allah have peace upon him – when she ran after her husband, after he had left her with her son in a sterile land! She repeatedly asked him: "O Ibrahim, where are you going, leaving us in this deserted land?" As she realised that he was not to give her an answer, she asked: "Has Allah commanded to do so?" He replied: "Yes." Then she said: "Allah will forsake us." Indeed, Allah does not forsake His righteous servants. Did Allah not compensate the man and his wife as mentioned in Surat al-Kahf:

❴As for the boy, his parents were believers, and we feared that he would oppress them by rebellion and disbelief. So we intended that their Lord would change him for them for one better in righteousness and nearer to mercy.❵ [1]

Did Allah not safeguard the treasure of the pious man for his two sons, when he ordered the companion of Musa ﷺ to build the wall again, in order to conceal it until the two boys grew up to take their father's treasure?

---

[1] Surat al-Kahf, Verse 80-81.

❨As for the wall, it belonged to the two orphan boys in the town, and there was under it a treasure belonging to them, and their father was a righteous man, and your Lord intended that they should attain their age of full strength, before they took out their treasure as a mercy from your Lord❩[1]

> *"I can neither change the past nor predict the future, so why should I regret or worry about anything?"*

---

[1] Surat al-Kahf, Verse 82.

8
Do not feel sorry about this world

Any person who recognizes the shortness of the time of this world, the modesty of its product, the vileness of its morals and its quick change against its people, will not feel sorry about missing anything of it. Therefore, do not feel sad about missing or losing anything in this world, for we have another world, which is greater, lasting and better than this one. It is the world of the Hereafter.

Praise Allah 🕮 that you are a believer in the meeting with the One God, Allah, while other non-Muslim women do not believe in this Promised Appointment with Him 🕮.

Congratulations to those who believe in the coming of that Day (the Last Day) and prepare for it.

Wretched is the one with weaker faith who forgets about this Day, and dedicates his life to his wealth and property, which are cheap products as compared to what is in store for the believers in the Hereafter.

What is the value of a mansion and jewellery when there is lack of faith?

What is the value of a high position in society when there is no fear of Allah?

If kingship, leadership and wealth could buy happiness, we would not see many kings, leaders or wealthy people living a life of distress, worry and anxiety!

> *"Yesterday is a finished dream, tomorrow is a sweet hope, but today is real."*

9
The delight of beauty is in Allah's Creation

L ook at man and the wonderful creation he represents, the diversity of his race, the multiplicity of his language and the variety of his nature. Allah ﷻ has created him in the most beautiful image:

❴...and (Allah) has formed you, giving you the best of forms❵[1]
❴O man, what has deceived you about your Lord, the Most Gracious, who created you, proportioned you and balanced you?❵[2]
❴Verily, We have created man in the best form❵[3]

Look at the awesome image of the sky, the perfect visage of the stars, the beauty of the sun, the emanation of the moon, and the vastness of the universe. Look at the earth and how Allah ﷻ unfolded it, and placed upon it its water and pasture. Look at the mountains and how He ﷻ firmly fixed them. Look at the wonderful nature of the seas, the rivers, the night, the day, light and the shades. Think about the secret harmony between all elements of this universe.

Look at this flower, damasked rose, seasoned fruit, delicious milk, sweet honey, palm tree, and this bee, ant, insect, and

---

[1] Surat Ghafir, Verse 64.
[2] Surat al-Infitar, Verse 6-7.
[3] Surat at-Tin, Verse 4.

fish. Look at these singing birds, these nightingales, these reptiles and other wondrous animals. It is a never-ending beauty and a delight for the eye.

❨So glory be to Allah when you start the night and when you greet the day. Praise to Him in the heavens and the earth, in the afternoon and when you reach midday. He brings forth the living from the dead and brings forth the dead from the living, and brings the earth after it was dead. In the same, you too will be brought forth.❩[1]

> *"Ignore the negative sides of the life; rather make use of its pleasures."*

---

[1] Surat ar-Rum, Verses 17-19.

10
The utmost kindness and endless generosity

When the Romans took some Muslim women prisoners, people informed Al-Mansour ibn 'Ammar and advised him to take a seat near the Amir of the believers (the Caliph) and urge people to invade the Roman Empire. So he went and managed to sit close to the Caliph, Harun Al-Rashid, in one of his gatherings in a place, called Al-Raqqah, near Damascus.

As Sheikh Mansour started urging people to do jihad in the path of Allah ﷻ, a folded piece of cloth with a letter attached to it was thrown to him. The Sheikh opened the letter and read:

I am a woman from the Arab clans, the news came to me about the detention of Muslim women by the Romans, and I have heard about your urge for people to invade them for that. I thought about the most praiseworthy thing in my body, namely my two braids, so I cut them and enclosed them in this folded piece of cloth. I urge you by Almighty Allah to use them as a bridle for a horse that is fighting for the Path of Allah, in the hope that Allah ﷻ may look at me in this condition and bestow His Mercy upon me."

Sheikh Mansour could not control himself after reading those deep expressions, so he wept and made everyone in the

---

[1] Surat al-Ahzab, Verse 33.

gathering weep with him. Then Harun Al-Rashid stood up and made a general call to arms. He mobilized the army of Mujahideen and participated himself in the holy fight, and Allah ﷻ made them victorious.

> *"Do not weep about what has gone; do not waste your tears; for you are not able to bring back the past."*

CHAPTER 8

{Only in the remembrance of Allah do hearts find peace.}[1]

1
You rely only on Allah ﷻ

A man entered the mosque before the time for the prescribed prayer, and found a ten-year old boy performing a prayer with humbleness and humility. He waited until the youngster finished his prayer and went to greet him and asked him: "O son, who are your parents?" The youngster bowed his head and a tear went down his cheek, then he lifted his head and said: "Sir, I am an orphan, who neither has a father nor a mother."

The man was touched by the reply of the youngster, so he said to him: "Would you like to be my son?" The boy asked: "But if I get hungry would you feed me? The man replied: "Yes." The boy asked: "If I am naked would you clothe me?" The man replied: "Yes." The boy asked: "If I am ill would you cure me? The man replied: "I am not able to do that, my son." The boy asked: "If I am dead, would you bring me back to life?" The man replied: "I am not able to do that."

The boy said: "Then Sir, leave me to the One Who created me, for He will guide me; the One Who gives me food and

---

[1] Surat ar-Ra'd, Verse 28.

drink, and when I am ill, He heals me; the One Who I hope will forgive me my sins, on the Day of Judgment."

The man stood silent for a moment, then he went away, saying: "I believe in Allah ﷻ, Whoever relies on Allah Alone, He will suffice him."

> *"No matter how hard you pull your hair or allow yourself to be overwhelmed by grief and sorrow, you will never be able to bring back a past event."*

2
Happiness exists, but who can find it?

Man can extract happiness only from within himself. However, he should adopt the right way to reach it. This right way is summed up in the following points:

He should be a truthful and brave person who loves his work and loves people.
He should love to cooperate with others and not be selfish.
He should be above all a conscientious person.

Happiness is not a myth; it is a clear reality. Many people enjoy it, and it is in our ability to enjoy it, if we learn from our past experiences, and benefit from the knowledge we have gained in our life.

If we look with insight into our life, we should be able to extract many things from ourselves. We can overcome many mental and physical diseases with knowledge, determination and patience, so that we live the life granted to us by Allah ﷻ, without ingratitude, disobedience or misery.

> *"The arch enemy of a woman's beauty is anxiety, which makes her look older than she is."*

---

[1] Surat al-A'raf, Verse 156.

3
Good character is a treasure in one's heart

People represent a mirror of each other. If one displays a good character with others, they will behave well with him, and so his nerves calm down and he will feel that he lives in a friendly society.

If, however, a person has a bad character, he will experience only bad morals and harshness from other people, because whoever does not respect others will no be respected.

A person with a good character is the one who is closer to peace of mind and far away from anxiety, distress and painful situations. Having a good character is an act of worship, which is vigorously advocated by Allah 🕮 and His Messenger 🕮. Allah 🕮 says:

{Show forgiveness, enjoy what is good, and turn away from the ignorant}[2]

{It is part of the Mercy of Allah that you deal gently with them. Were you severe or harsh-hearted they would have broken away from you; so pass over (their faults) and ask for Allah's Forgiveness for them; and consult them in affairs (of moment). Then when thou have taken a

---

[1] Surat Ad-Duha, Verse 5.
[2] Surat al-A'raf, Verse 199.

decision put your trust in Allah. Allah loves those who put their trust in Him.⟩[1]

The Prophet ﷺ said: *"The most beloved of you to me are those who are best in character and humble, who get along with people and people get along with them. The most disliked of you to me are those who walk around spreading malicious gossip, and causing division between friends, those who seek out the faults of the innocent."*

> *"Hesitation, slackness and treating a problem without hope lead people to a nervous breakdown."*

---

[1] Surat Al-'Imran, Verse 159.

{Allah does not burden a soul beyond its scope.}[1]

4
The ten articles of happiness

D Dicks, an American psychologist said: "A happy life is a fine art which has ten tips, and they are:

1- Practise a work that you like, and if it is not possible for you, then practise a hobby which you like in your free time and devote yourself to it.

2- Take care of your health, for it is the spirit of happiness. This requires from you to be moderate in eating and drinking, to practise some sport regularly and to give up harmful habits.

3- There should be a purpose in your life, for it will grant you self-sacrifice and motivation.

4- Take life as it comes with its sweet and bitter gifts.

5- Man should live his present life, without regret over his past or anxiety about his future.

6- Man should think hard about his work and decisions, and should not blame others about the consequences of his decisions.

7- Man should look at those who are in a worse state than him.

---

[1] Surat al-Baqarah, Verse 286.

8- Man should be always cheerful and in the company of bright people.

9- Man should endeavour to make others happy to benefit from that happiness.

10- Take advantage of happy hours and use them as a necessary platform of cheerfulness.

"Enjoy your day and make the most of it. Look for anything that will prevent harm before it takes place."

⟨Everyday He is engaged in some affairs⟩[1]

5
Seek refuge with Allah from anxiety and grief

I do not think that a wise man would lack cheerfulness or a believer would surrender to pessimism and despair. Sometimes, a person could go through hard times and lack peace of mind and tranquillity; therefore, he should adhere to the Guidance of Allah ﷻ Who will save him from his ordeal, because any surrender to depression would be the beginning of the collapse of one's will and would characterise all deeds with failure and disappointment.

The Prophet ﷺ used to teach his Companions to seek Allah's Help to overcome their hardships. Abu Sa'id Al-Khudri ﵁ said: "One day the Messenger of Allah ﷺ entered the mosque. He saw there a man from the Ansar called Abu Umamah and said to him: 'What is the matter that I am seeing you sitting in the mosque when there is no time of prayer?' Abu Umamah replied: 'I am entangled in worries and debts, O Messenger of Allah.' The Prophet ﷺ said: 'Shall I not teach you words by which, when you say them, Allah will remove your worry and settle your debt?' Abu Umamah replied: 'Why not, O Messenger of Allah?' He ﷺ said: 'Say in the morning and evening: 'O Allah, I seek refuge in You from worry and grief, I seek refuge in You from incapacity and slackness, I seek refuge in You from cowardice and niggardliness, and I seek in You from being overcome by debt and being put in subjection by men.' Abu

---

[1] Surat ar-Rahman, Verse 29.

Umamah said: 'When I did that Allah removed my worry and settled my debt."[1]

> *"Ulcer's pain does not come from what you eat, but rather from what eats you."*

---

[1] Recorded by Abu Dawud.

6
The woman who is a good support in time of calamities

It was narrated in the biography of our ancestors that Fatimah, daughter of the Prophet ﷺ used to endure many days of hunger. Her husband, 'Ali ibn Abi Talib ﷺ, noticed one day the paleness of her face, so he said to her: "What is the matter with you, O Fatimah?" She replied: "We have gone three days without having food in our house!"

He ﷺ said: "Why did you not tell me?" She replied: "My father, the Messenger of Allah ﷺ, said to me, on my wedding night: "O Fatimah, if Ali brings you something, then eat, otherwise, do not ask him about it!"

However, many women's concern is to empty their husbands' pockets. They would not bear to see money with their husbands and not with them; they would make a big fuss until they get hold of it.

There is no doubt that when a man surrenders once to his wife's excessive demands, he will make a stand one day, and this will lead to constant disputes, which may result in divorce.

"Life is too short to make it shorter,
so do not try to shorten it further."

---

¹ Surat an-Nahl, Verse 53.

7

A woman from the people of Paradise

'Ata' ibn Abi Rabah ﷺ reported that ibn 'Abbas ﷺ said to him: "Shall I show a woman from the people of Paradise?" I said: "Yes." He said: "It is this black woman; she came to the Messenger of Allah ﷺ and said: 'I get attacks of epilepsy and my body becomes uncovered; please invoke Allah for me.' The Prophet ﷺ said to her: 'If you wish, be patient and you will be rewarded with entry to Paradise; and if you wish, I will invoke Allah to cure you.' She said: 'I will remain patient,' and added, 'but I become uncovered, so please invoke Allah for me that I may not become uncovered.' The Prophet ﷺ invoked Allah for her."[1]

This pious believing woman accepted her suffering in this world, in return for entry to Paradise, and she gained a good deal indeed. Nevertheless, she refused to be uncovered when she is stricken with epilepsy, because such indecent condition does not fit a righteous Muslim woman. So what should we say to those women who are dressed yet seem naked, who spare no effort in displaying their beauty and adornment; thus removing all signs of decency?

> *"Stop worrying. Be firm in facing your real world."*

---

[1] Recorded by al-Bukhari.

8
Charity wards off tribulation

C harity is a great way to experience patience and peace of mind. Good deeds are rewarded by Allah ﷻ, in this life, with a feeling of bliss, delight and gratification.

Give charity, even if it is a small amount. Do not belittle anything you offer as charity, be it a date, a glass of water or milk. Give to the destitute and the miserable. Feed the hungry and visit the sick. It is then that you will feel that Allah ﷻ has reduced your worries and sorrows. Charity is a medicine that exists only in the "pharmacy" of Islam.

A man asked the Imam Abdullah ibn Al-Mubarak: "O Abu Abdu-Rahman, I have been suffering from an injury to my knee for seven years now. I have asked the doctors, and received many treatments, but the pain is still there."

Ibn Al-Mubarak said to him: "Go and look for a place where people are desperate for water, and dig a well for them. I hope that water gushes forth from that well and so the bleeding in your knee will stop." The man did accordingly and his injury was cured.

There is nothing strange in this story, O dear sister; for the Prophet ﷺ said: "Treat your ill people with charity" and he ﷺ also said: "Charity extinguishes Allah's Anger and wards off a bad ending."

"Anxiety is the dear companion of idleness."

9
Be cheerful because the universe is beautiful

There is no doubt that the image of the stars in the sky is so beautiful; an overwhelming beauty indeed, with variant characteristics according to the changes of time; from morning to evening, from sunset to sunrise, from moonlit night to a dark night, and from clear sky to a cloudy one. This image sometimes changes from one hour to another and from one corner to another. It is all a beautiful and breathtaking scene.

The lonely beautiful star, which blinks in the sky looks like a beautiful eye which shines with love; while the two separate stars move away from the crowd, as if they want to have a private talk! The group of stars scattered around display the scene of a night festival in the sky.

The moon either seems dreaming one night or wandering the other. It is sometimes radiant and sometimes dimmed; sometimes it is newly born and sometimes fading away.

The eye neither wears out staring at this vast universe nor can it reach its spacious end.

---

[1] Surat ar-Rahman, Verse 72.

This is the definition of beauty, which man can live and witness, but cannot truly describe it with the words and expressions he has!

> *"It is necessary to accept one's real world which is inevitable, and there is no need to worry as it is pointless."*

{Do not display yourselves as it was previously displayed in the time of ignorance}[1]

10
A brave woman

The Amir of the believers, 'Uthman ibn 'Affan ﷺ, appointed Habib ibn Maslmah Al-Fihri as leader of the Muslim army to invade the Romans, who had challenged the Muslims.

The wife of Habib was also included in the army, and before the battle started, Habib ﷺ began checking the positions of his soldiers, when his wife asked him: "Where shall I find you when fighting intensifies?"

He replied: "You will either find me in the tent of the Roman leader or in Paradise!" The war raged on. Habib and his soldiers fought vigorously in a manner never witnessed before, and Allah ﷻ made them victorious over the Romans.

Habib ﷺ rushed to the tent of the Roman leader to wait for his wife, only to find her there – to his amazement – as she preceded him.

"There is nothing difficult or impossible in life, as long as there is ability and action."

---

[1] Surat al-Ahzab, Verse 33.

CHAPTER 9

{So remember Me and I will remember you}[1]

1
Do not waste your time

The Prophet ﷺ said to 'Aishah ﷺ: "If you commit a sin, then ask Allah ﷺ for forgiveness and repent to Him. For if a person acknowledges his sin and repents, Allah will accept his repentance."

Imagine that you have achieved all your wishes and dreams, and then all of a sudden, you have lost everything. You will then cry and feel a great deal of pain; you will bite your fingers out of remorse and regret. So what about your life which slips away from you, while you are unaware of it?

Your life is a precious jewel, which cannot be valued materially. This life is in reality a set of breaths, which once out of the body will never come back.

These breaths are your capital in life. You are able to buy anything with them whatever you desire of the pleasures of Paradise; so how can you waste this life without a sincere repentance?

> *"There is one way leading to happiness; that is to stop worrying about things beyond our control."*

---

[1] Surat al-Baqarah, Verse 152.

131

2
Happiness cannot be bought with money

Many people have spent their youth and health for the sake of accumulating money, then they spent all their life spending what they had earned to gain happiness, but they received only misery. They tried to regain their youth, but were overwhelmed by old age; they desired to have good health, but were defeated by incurable diseases!

A famous actor once said that his one wish in life was to make money. He thought that he could be the happiest man in the world with his wealth for a whole century! He was certain that he could achieve all his desires with his money.

After a period of twenty years, Allah ﷻ made him earn a fortune, which was double what he had wished, but took away his health, youth and dreams!

It was reported that he used to weep, saying: "I wish I had never asked Allah for money. I wish I had asked Allah to live a hundred years in poverty, eating only baked beans and sneaking onto the tram to avoid paying the fare!

This actor never knew the value of good health, until he missed it. He never learnt that money cannot buy

---

¹ Surat al-Baqarah, Verse 137.

everything, until he became the wealthiest artist in Egypt, and discovered that he could not add a single day to his ending life with all his fortune!

> *"One should not waste half one's life in disputes."*

3
Haste and carelessness generate misery

Forbearance is a quality of valour with which man overcomes his anger and foolish desires, while deliberation is a quality of certainty, great patience and use of wisdom.

These two characteristics stand against anxiety. Whoever lacks them indeed lacks a great deal of good, and is likely to remain a victim of worry.

A forbearing person holds off a lot of evils, whereas the imprudent gives way to his anger and lets anxiety take over him.

A wise person rarely regrets his actions or indulges in matters with unknown consequences. But the hasty and silly person suffers constant worry, anxiety and bad results.

Similarly, when a person is kind to himself and dutiful to others, he is always successful, thanks to his calmness and peace of mind.

Our pure Islamic religion encourages kindness, forbearance and deliberation. The Prophet ﷺ said: "Kindness is not to be

---

[1] Surat al-Baqarah, Verse 45.

found in anything but that it adds to its beauty and it is not withdrawn from anything but it makes it defective."[1]

"We waste the time of our happiness in this life for the sake of insignificant things."

[1] Recorded by Muslim.

135

4
Accumulating wealth has no end

Beaver Brook said: "I have accumulated a lot of money, but I realised, from my experience, that progressing in this process – the process of making money – is dangerous; it has no end and it consumes one's life and happiness. It is for this reason that I have changed my work and opted for something I desire in the publication field, which does not generate a great deal of money; yet it brings happiness to me in the service of society.

I advise every businessman who has made a fortune to give up such activity and retire early so that he can enjoy his achievements, and to start a new desired activity, in which he enjoys his time in the service of his society.

A wealthy person who has accumulated and earned a great fortune shows less interest about leaving his huge fortune to his inheritors, because he knows that they will be better if they get into the field without such a fortune, and with only their intellect and morals to work for them.

A wealth gained without any effort usually becomes a curse not a blessing, a misery not happiness; as inheritors meet their demands and low desires in luxury and laziness, filling

---

[1] Surat al-Haj, Verse 78.

their minds with silly and useless ideas, and wasting their youth to no end.

"You should firmly believe that nothing is impossible in this life"

5
It is in idleness that immorality is born

I t is in the circle of unemployment that many immoral acts are born. If work is the message of the living, then the unemployed are dead.

If our present life is a grounding for a greater subsequent life, then the idle people are most likely to end up bankrupt, with only doom and failure as their capital.

The Prophet ﷺ informed about the heedlessness of thousands who were granted the blessing of health and leisure, saying: "There are two blessings of which people are careless: good health and free time."

Indeed, many healthy people struggle in this life without any goal ahead or any activity to occupy their times, or any message to carry out.

Is man created for this idleness? Not at all. Allah ﷻ says:

⟨Did you then think that We had created you in jest and that you would not be brought back to Us (for account)? Therefore Exalted be Allah, the King, the Truth; there is no god but He, the Lord of the Throne of Honour!⟩²

---

¹ Surat al-Anbiya', Verse 69.
² Surat al-Mu'minun, Verses 115-116.

Life was created with the truth, and so were the earth, the heavens and everything between them. Therefore, man, as part of this world, should be acquainted with this truth and live with it.

But if he confines himself to the circle of his low desires, then he has made a bad choice for his present and his future.

> *"Always picture the image of success in your mind."*

6
A house where there is neither anger, noise nor trouble

She said to her father, weeping: "O father, there was a dispute between me and my husband yesterday, and he got angry for a word I said. When I saw him angry, I regretted what I said, and apologized to him; but he refused to talk to me, and turned his face away. I kept on apologizing until he laughed and accepted.

I am worried that Allah ﷻ will hold me accountable for the incident in which I stirred my husband's anger."

Her father said to her: "O daughter, had you died before your husband was pleased with you, I would not have been pleased with you. Do you not know that any woman whose husband is angry with her is cursed in the Torah, the Bible and the Qur'an, that the throes of death will be even harder for her and that her grave will be made narrow for her? So, glad news for a woman whose husband is pleased with her!"

The righteous woman is keen to be loved by her husband; so she is always careful not to spoil the good spirits in their life.
"Chase away the feeling of failure and keep its image out of your mind."

---

[1] Surat at-Talaq, Verse 3.

7

Chastity and modesty add to the prettiness of the most beautiful

Have you heard of the story of Umm Salamah, the wife of the Prophet ﷺ, when she heard him, saying: "Whoever drags his garment on the floor out of pride, Allah will not look at him on the Day of Judgment?" so she asked: "What should women do with their garment hems?" the Prophet ﷺ replied: "Extend them by a span of the hand" she said: "But their feet will be uncovered." He ﷺ replied: "Extend them by a cubit, but no more than that."

What a good example was the Mother of the believers, Umm Salamah, who was not one of the arrogant or proud people!

Believing women are chaste and modest, purified and honoured. Even their feet should not be seen; they let their garments drag over their feet, so that men do not see anything of them.

But women in our time – apart from those under the Mercy of Allah ﷺ - instead lift their dress as high as they can, lest they get dirty, and if they could they would take it off, in the same manner as the disbelieving women and the common prostitutes. They come out with thousands of reasons for their nakedness, while their shameless husbands walk alongside them, with utmost carelessness.

> *"Eating less food provides good health, committing less sins gives peace of mind, worrying less helps appease the heart, whilst talking little safeguards one's tongue."*

"The steadfast always gets the bets offers."

8
Allah ﷻ may bring back the absent

After a separation, which lasted more than twenty years, it was decreed by Allah ﷻ - in a very strange story – that a woman be joined again by her twenty-five year old daughter. Life circumstances had led to their separation, but they were finally together when the daughter was spending her honeymoon in the mountains of the Sawdah resort in Abha.

The mother had remarried after her husband had divorced her and her daughter was then three years old. Her new husband's lifestyle and his regular transfers from one country to another had prevented her from seeing her daughter who remained in the care of her father.

During one beautiful summer day, in the mountains of Sawdah, the daughter met a woman in the resort, and they began chatting, while no one knew the other before. As they continued talking to each other, the woman noticed that one of the girl's fingers was missing, so she asked her about her mother.

The daughter told her her story. The woman was surprised to see herself face to face with her daughter, whom she had lost for twenty years. She hugged her and kissed her with the love and affection of a mother, expressing how much she had missed her all those past years.

"Thinking of happiness definitely leads to thinking of the past and the future, and this in itself spoils the feeling of happiness."

9
A word which fills the time and the place

Musa ﷽ said: "O Lord, Teach me a supplication with which I will call you and converse with you." Allah ﷻ says: "O Musa, say: "La Ilaha illa Allah (There is no god but Allah)." Musa ﷽ said: "All people say La Ilaha illa Allah (There is no god but Allah)." Allah ﷻ said: "O Musa, if the seven heavens and the earth were to be placed on one side of the scale and 'La Ilaha illa Allah' on the other, 'La Ilaha illa Allah' would outweigh them."

'La Ilaha illa Allah' (There is no god but Allah) has shining lights; it removes all aspects of sins according to the power and weakness of its light. It has a light, but its power varies in people's hearts, and only Allah ﷻ knows its degree in them.

There are people whose hearts shine with this word like the sun, a striking star, while in others, it makes their hearts shine less like a dim one.

As the light of this word becomes brighter, the desires to commit sins become weaker.

"Happiness of the believer lies in his love of Allah ﷻ Love for the sake of Allah instils a deep happiness,

---

¹ Surat ar-Rahman, Verse 58.

witnessed only by sincere believers, who reject any other alternative for it."

10
Hearts that longed for Paradise

Have you heard the story of the woman, whose husband Salih ibn Huyay died and left her with their two sons? She brought them up alone and the first thing she taught them was the way to worship Allah ﷻ, to be obedient and to be accustomed in performing the night prayer.

She said to her sons: "We should not let one moment of a night slip by without any one of us standing in prayer and remembering Allah ﷻ." They said: "What do you mean, mother?" She replied: "We shall divide the night into three parts between us. One of you to stand in prayer during the first part; the other stand in prayer in the second part, and I will stand in prayer in the third and last part, then I will wake you up for the dawn prayer."
They said: "We hear and we obey, O Mother!"

When the mother died, the two sons never gave up the night prayer, because devotion and worship of Allah ﷻ had filled their hearts. In fact, their best moments in life were those spent standing in prayer at night.

They divided the night between the two of them. When one of them was felt very ill, the other stood in prayer all night alone.

"Life around us with its beautiful and noble image is a true invitation to happiness"

CHAPTER 10

If you tried to number the blessings of Allah, you could never count them [1]

1
Belief in the Divine Decree, both its good and bad

Allah ﷺ says:

No misfortune can happen on earth or in your souls but is recorded in a decree before We bring it into existence: that is truly easy for Allah [2]

But it is possible that you dislike a thing which is good for you and that you love a thing which is bad for you. But Allah knows and you do not know [3]

Belief in fate and divine decree plays a significant role in drawing peace to the mind of the stricken person, especially when the person believes in the fact that Allah ﷺ is Compassionate to His Slaves and wants ease for them, and that He ﷺ is wise and All-Knowing who keeps rewards for

---

[1] Surat Ibrahim, Verse 34.
[2] Surat al-Hadid, Verse 22-23.
[3] Surat al-Baqarah, Verse 216.

them in the Hereafter, to eventually give in abundance to the patient.

When a person ponders on this fact and implements it, it turns the grief and sorrow into joy and happiness, however, not everyone is capable to do it.

So, what are the steps that you follow in order to ease the misfortunes and tragedies of the mind?

1- Imagine the misfortune as being worse than it actually is.
2- Consider the state of the one whose calamity is greater and more painful.
3- Look at the blessings that you are enjoying, while many people are deprived.
4- Do not give in to despair which accompanies a calamity
5- Remember that Allah ﷻ says: ﴿**Verily, along with every hardship there is relief. Verily, along with every hardship there is relief** ﴾[1]

> *"Among the quickest messages of happiness to the minds of others is a sincere smile from the heart."*

---

[1] Surat al-'Asr, Verse 5.

《None besides Allah can avert it (i.e. the Day of Resurrection)》[1]

2
The best things are moderate ones

Mustafa Mahmoud said: "I feel happy because I am a common man. My income is average, my health is typical, and my standard of life is normal. I have a little of everything, which means that I have a lot of motivations. In fact motivation is life itself.

Motivations in our hearts are the real impetus of life, and they are the basis by which we assess our happiness.

I call on Allah ﷻ to grant the reader of these lines an ordinary life, to give him a little of everything, and it is by Allah a good prayer.

My mother did not understand philosophy, yet she possessed a pure nature, which enabled her to perceive the meaning of all these words, without reading them. She used to call it a simple but meaningful name: Al-Sitr (the shield); a little of everything but plenty of spirit.

> *"A false smile is a clear image of hypocrisy."*

---

[1] Surat an-Najm, Verse 58.

The Prophet ﷺ said: "My delight of the eye was made in prayer."

3
Pessimism invites depression

A person always has an effect upon his companion and his morals. If the companion – a friend or life-partner or colleague – is calm, cheerful, laid-back and optimistic in his life, then he will likely transfer these good attributes to his companion.

But if he is grim-faced, gloomy, miserable, constantly nervous and pessimistic, then he will definitely spread his dark attitude around his companion and adversely affect him.

Companionship is not confined to people. There are also other companions affecting man, such as books and media programmes; they include the optimistic and the pessimistic, the anxious and the calm.

Books are annual seasons; they comprise spring and autumn. If man is successful in selecting bright books, which encourage serenity, success and self-confidence, then he would do himself a favour and open shining windows of delight and happiness.

But if he picks books of misery and anxiety, which doubt all values and human nature and are pessimistic about life and mankind, then it may contagiously affect him, as a disease affects a healthy person, and may ruin his life.

"The way to happiness is in front of you. So seek it by means of

knowledge, righteous deeds and good character. Be moderate in all your affairs and you will be happy."

4

Avoid vexation and discontent

An experienced man once said: "When I was in my twenties and thirties, I used to complain and moan about everything, despite that I was enjoying myself, because I ignored the meaning of happiness. I did not know tat I was indeed living in happiness.

Now that I am over sixty, I certainly know how I was very happy in my twenties and thirties.
However, it is a knowledge that came too late; mere memories and regrettable ones indeed.

If only I perceived it then, I would have lived with greater delight. There would have been no room for complaint or discontent in my youth.

Dear reader, you either live your happiness with cheerfulness, delighting all your senses with its open roses before you, or you ignore it, turning to what you are lacking and showing your anger and discontent; then you wait until your present becomes your past and you will regret your carelessness. You will then understand that you were once very happy, but you did not know it at that time, and all you have in your hands are bad memories!

> *"A woman may turn her house into a Paradise or may turn it into an unbearable hell!"*

---

[1] Surat al-Fath, Verse 18.

5

Most problems are caused by trivialities

Unfortunately, many silly incidents make thousands of people lose their common sense, separate families and break relationships, and leave them hopeless and confused in their life.

Dale Carnegie explains the consequences of the rashness to deal with trivial issues, and says: "Minor incidents which take place in marital lives can make spouses lose their senses, and cause half the heart problems in the world."

At least this has been confirmed by experts. Joseph Sabath, a Chicago judge who had dealt with more than forty thousand divorce cases, said: "You usually find silly incidents behind every misery that strikes a marriage."

Frank Hogan, public prosecutor in New York, said: "Half the cases which are presented in criminal courts are caused by minor incidents; such as an argument between members of a family, a passing insult, hurtful abuse or an abusive gesture. It is these trivial incidents that lead to killings or other crimes."

---

[1] Surat al-Ma'idah, Verse 119.

Very few of us are harsh by nature, but constant aggression directed to our pride and dignity is the reason behind half the problems suffered in the world.

"The greatest blessing which should be cared for is goodness, when it fills one's mind and delights one's life."

﴾*Remember when you sought help of your Lord and He answered you*﴿[1]

6
The art of preserving one's tongue

An historian reported that Khalid ibn Yazeed ibn Mu'awiyah slandered 'Abdullah ibn Al-Zubayr, the arch enemy of Banu Umayyah, describing him as a miser. His wife, Ramlah bint Al-Zubayr – the sister of Abdullah – was sitting in the gathering and did not say a word. So Khalid said to her: "Why do you not say anything? Is it an approval of what I just said or a decision not to answer me?

She replied: "Neither this nor that! But a woman was not created to interfere in the affairs of men. Rather we are flowers to be smelled and hugged. Why should we stick our nose into your matters?" He was pleased with her answer and kissed her between her eyes.

---

[1] Surat al-Anfal, Verse 9.

The Prophet ﷺ firmly forbade the revelation of secrets between spouses. The Imam Ahmad ibn Hanbal reported a narration from Asm'a bint Yazeed that she attended a gathering of the Prophet ﷺ, while men and women were sitting there, and he ﷺ said: "Maybe a man says what he does with his wife, and maybe a woman says what she does with her husband." Everyone in the gathering kept silent; so I said: "By Allah, yes they do, O Messenger of Allah!" the Prophet ﷺ then said: "Do not do it. It is as if a male devil met a female devil on the road and he has intercourse with her while people are looking at them!"

The interpreters of the Qur'an interpreted the word "Hafidhat (women who guard)" in the Verse: ❨**Therefore the righteous women are devoutly obedient, and guard in the husband's absence what Allah orders them to guard**❩[1] as the women who guard the secrets of everything happening between them and their husbands.

> *"Instead of counting your problems, count the blessings of Allah ﷻ upon you."*

---

[1] Surat an-Nisa', Verse 34.

"Life is short, so do not make it even shorter with your worries."

7
Fight worry with Salat

The first Muslim women knew that Salat is the link between a person and his Lord, and that those who pray with devotion and humbleness are made successful.

Allah ﷻ says: ❨**Successful indeed are the believers. Those who offer Salat with all solemnity and full submissiveness**❩[1]

They used to stand their nights praying with humility; they knew that one of the best provisions for the Hereafter and the one that helps the Message of Islam reach people is Salat, which grants its performer a power and determination to overcome hardships and difficulties. They knew performing the night prayer is one of the best acts of worship of Allah ﷻ, Who says, addressing the Prophet ﷺ: ❨**In some parts of the night, offer the Salat with it (the Qur'an) as an additional prayer; it may be that your Lord will raise you to a station of praise and glory**❩[2] Allah ﷻ also says, praising those who perform the night prayer:❨**They used to sleep but little of the night**❩[3]

---

[1] Surat al-Mu'minun, Verse 1-2.
[2] Surat al-Isra', Verse 79.
[3] Surat adh-Dhariyat, Verse 17.

Anas ibn Malik ﷺ reported that once the Prophet ﷺ entered the Mosque and saw a rope hanging between its two pillars. He said: "What is this rope?" The people said: "This rope is for Zainab who, when she feels tired, holds it (to keep standing for the prayer.)" The Prophet ﷺ said: "Don't use it. Remove the rope. You should pray as long as you feel active, and when you get tired, sit down."[1]

Therefore, the believing women used to force themselves to pray at night in order to please Allah ﷻ. But the Prophet ﷺ ordered them not to perform beyond their ability; for the best act of worship is the one performed regularly even if it is a little.

We know that women in our time have filled all their times with worldly affairs, so they should content themselves with at least two rak'ahs (one optional Salat is made up of two rak'ahs) in the middle of the night to overcome the devil's whisperings.

The best of matters are the moderate ones, for the Prophet ﷺ said that those who perform worship in excess are doomed to fail.

> *"Put your trust in Allah if you are truthful, and rejoice for tomorrow if you are repentant."*

---

[1] Recorded by al-Bukhari.

8
Advice of a successful woman

A modern woman advised her daughter with following advice, mixed with her smile and tears: "O my daughter, you are about to start a new life, away from your parents and your brothers and sisters. In this new life, you will the partner to your husband, who would not like to share you with anyone, including those from your own flesh and blood.

Be his wife and mother. Make him feel that you are everything in his life and his world. Always remember that a man is like an overgrown boy who is delighted with smallest sweet word. Do not let him feel that by marrying you, he has deprived you of your family, for he is experiencing the same feeling as well; he has also left the house of his parents for your sake. However, the difference between you and him is the difference between a man and a woman. The woman always yearns for her family and the house in which she was born and brought up; but she has to accustom herself to her new life. It is necessary for her to settle in with the man who has become her husband, guardian and father of her children... this is your new world.

My daughter, this is your present and future. This is your family, which both you and your husband jointly created. I do not ask from you to forget your father, mother, brothers and sisters, because they will never forget you. How can a woman forget her own child? But I ask you to love your husband, to obey him and to rejoice in your life with him."

"Learn patience from Asiyah, loyalty from Khadijah, sincerity from 'Aishah, and firmness from Fatimah."

9
Whoever does not find comfort in Allah will not find comfort in anything else

Allah 繁 is the cause of consolation for the believer, the comfort of the obedient, and the beloved of the worshiper. Whoever finds comfort in Him will find comfort in life and will rejoice his living days. His heart feels peaceful and serene, as the love of Allah is firmly planted in it, the Attributes of Allah are settled in his mind. Indeed, he is mindful of Allah's Names, which he learns by heart. He ponders on such Attributes as: Al-Rahman (The Most Gracious), Al-Raheem (the Most Merciful), Al-Hameed (The Praiseworthy), Al-Haleem (The Forbearing), Al-Barr (The Most Kind), Al-Lateef (the Most Courteous), Al-Muhsin (The Most Beneficent), Al-Wadud (The Most Loving), Al-Kareem (The Most Generous), Al-'Adheem (The Almighty)... so he finds solace in Al-Baari (The Creator), loves the Al-'Adheem and feels the closeness of Al-'Aleem (The All-Knowing).

Feeling Allah's closeness to His slave necessitates finding Comfort in Him and delight for His Care. Allah 繁 says:

---

[1] Surat ar-Rahman, Verse 74.

162

❰When My slaves ask you about Me, I am indeed near to them (by My knowledge). I respond to the invocations of the supplicant when he calls on Me❱[1]

Finding comfort in Allah does not come without a reason and is not achieved without any strife for it. It is the result of constant obedience to Allah 🕮 and the result of the sincere love of Allah 🕮. Whoever obeys Allah 🕮, adheres to His Commands, avoids His Prohibitions and is sincere in his love of Him 🕮, then he will find joy and comfort in the Closeness of Allah 🕮 to him.

"Real beauty is one's character, ethics and mind."

---

[1] Surat al-Baqarah, Verse 186.

10

Asma', the women with the two straps, lived two lives

Asma', daughter of Abu Bakr, gave a good and dramatic example of patience over hardships and deprivation. She was extremely keen to obey her husband and always sought to please him.

She was reported as saying: "Al-Zubayr married me while he possessed only his horse. I used to clean and feed the horse. I crushed date pits, brought water and baked bread. I used to transport date pits from the land of Al-Zubayr, so the Prophet ﷺ invited me to mount behind him, but I was ashamed as I remembered Al-Zubayr and his jealousy. So the Prophet ﷺ went on, and when I returned home, I informed Al-Zubayr and he said: "By Allah, your carrying the date pits is harder on me than you riding behind him!" I stayed the course until Abu Bakr sent me a servant, who relieved me from looking after the horse, and I felt as if he had set me free."

After all this patience, she and her husband were showered with blessings, yet her character and attitude did not change because of her wealth. She was rather generous to the extent that she never stored anything for the future. If she felt ill, she would wait until she got better and then set all her slaves

---

[1] Recorded by al-Bukhari.

free. She used to say to her daughters and her family: "Give charity and do not wait until you have in abundance."

"Life is beautiful for the believers and the hereafter is beloved for the pious; they are the only happy ones."

CHAPTER 11

⟨Do not be distressed because of what they plot⟩[1]

1
Who is the most beloved?

You should love him more than all people!

Have you ever asked yourself how much do you love the Messenger of Allah? Do you know the reality of this love lies in implementing all that he commands and avoiding all that forbids?

Reconsider your emotions and direct the feeling of love – first and foremost – to Allah 🕮, then to the one (the Prophet 🕮) with whom Allah 🕮 saved us from misguidance.

If you want your rank in Paradise to be very high, remember the Hadith in which the Prophet 🕮 said: "A person will be with the one whom he loved."

However, one of the first signs of this love is the adherence to the teachings of the Prophet 🕮. How can anyone claim to love when he goes against his commands and does not follow his Sunnah?

---

[1] Surat an-Nahl, Verse 127.

Read the Prophet's biography to see how excellent was his character, how good were his words, how tolerant was his attitude and how submissive he was to Allah ﷻ

Change your character to be similar to his.

"The wives of Prophets Noah and Lot betrayed their faith so they were disgraced and punished, but Asiyah and Maryam believed and so they were honoured."

***(I am indeed near to them (by My knowledge). I respond to
the invocations of the supplicant when he calls on Me)**[1]*

2
Happiness is not a matter of riches or poverty

Bernard Shaw said: "I cannot say that I truly tasted poverty. Before I could earn anything from my writings, I used to own a great library, the public library in the British Museum. I also had an art exhibition place near Trafalgar Square. What could I do with the money? Smoke cigars? But I do not smoke. Drink champagne? But I do not drink. Buy thirty suits of the latest fashion, so that I would quickly be invited to dinner in their palaces? But I try to avoid meeting such people as much as possible. Buy horses? They are dangerous. Buy cars? I get annoyed with them.

Now that I have the money to buy all of these things, I still buy only the items which I used to buy when I was poor.

My happiness lies in the things which used to make me happy when I was poor: a book to read, a painting to scrutinize, an idea to write. On the other hand, I have a fresh imagination, and I cannot remember needing anything more than lying down, closing my eyes so that I picture myself roaming in the world of imagination as I like.

---

[1] Surat al-Baqarah, Verse 186.

168

So, what benefit do I got from the miserable luxury displayed in Bond Street?

"Make your house a garden of peace, not a field of noise, for tranquillity is a blessing."

3
Does Allah not deserve gratefulness more than anyone else?

Being grateful to Allah ﷻ is the most beautiful and easiest prescription of happiness and peace of mind, because when you thank your Lord, you think of His blessings upon you, and so you feel the extent of Allah's Grace upon you.

A rightly-guided predecessor used to say: "If you want to know Allah's blessing upon you, close your eyes." Think about Allah's blessings upon you, such as hearing, eyesight, intellect, religion, children, provisions and commodities.

Some women overlook all the blessings they dispose of, but if they look at those less fortunate women, such as the poor, destitute, wretched, ill and stricken women, they would have thanked Allah ﷻ for the blessings they enjoy, even if they lived in small tents or under a tree in the desert.

Praise Allah ﷻ for His blessings upon you, and compare your life with that of those who are stricken in their body,

---

¹ Surat at-Tahreem, Verse 11.

brain, hearing or children, and there are many of them in this world.

> *"Give a word of comfort to women who lost their children, and wipe away the tears of the wretched with an acceptable charity."*

4
A happy woman makes a cheerful environment

Orison Sweet said: "Napoleon was fortunate to marry the Empress Josephine before he assumed the top leadership and faced the challenges of his conquests. Her gentle attitude and pleasant character were stronger than the loyalty of dozens of men to earn him the allegiance of his followers.

She used to spread happiness around her. She never gave orders directly, even to her servants; she explained her attitude to one of her friends, saying: "I use the phrase "I want" only in one context in which I say: I want everyone around me to be happy." It was as if the English poet was referring to her when he said: "She passed by the road on a happy morning and the morning glory spread throughout the day."

In reality, kindness extends happiness among us and among those around us, even static objects. Kindness is an abstract beauty, which has no limit; it is to man like beauty is to women. As for women, it increases their beauty.

"Is she happy, the woman who displays her beauty and adornment to evil people?"

"Acknowledge Allah ﷻ in times of ease, He will support you in times of hardship."

5
Be calm, for everything goes according to Divine Decree

Instead of belief in the fate of divine decree, Dale Carnegie requires from a stricken person not to resist his calamity and freeze like a buffalo or tree roots! He may be excused for his suggestion because he has not come across the cure which is in our hands.

He said: "I once refused to accept an inevitable situation with which I was confronted. I played the fool and railed against it, and rebelled. I turned my nights into hells of insomnia. I brought upon myself everything I did not want. Finally, after a year of self-torture, I had to accept what I knew from the outset I could not possibly alter. I should have cried out years ago with old Walt Whitman:

> Oh, to confront night, storms, hunger
> ridicule, accident, rebuttal
> as the trees and animals do.

I spent twelve years working with cattle; yet I never saw a Jersey cow running a temperature because the pasture was burning up from a lack of rain or because of sleet and cold or because her boyfriend was paying too much attention to another heifer. The animals confront night, storms, and hunger calmly; so they never have nervous breakdowns or stomach ulcers!"

"Remember success and happy events, and forget about calamities and distressful times."

6
Umm 'Amarah speaks

Nusaybah bint Ka'b (Umm 'Amarah) reported the story of the Battle of Uhud, saying: "I went out early in the day to check on people, carrying water, until I reached the Messenger of Allah ﷺ who was with his Companions, who were winning the battle at the time. But when the Muslims were defeated at the end, I joined the section of the Prophet ﷺ and I started fighting with a sword and throwing arrows, until I was wounded.

When people left the Messenger of Allah, ibn Qamee'ah came forward, saying: "Where is Muhammad? I will not live if he stays safe!"

So I confronted him with Mus'ab ibn 'Umayr, but he struck me on my shoulder, after I gave a series of blows; as the enemy of Allah had two body armours!"

This was Umm 'Amarah, on whom the Prophet ﷺ said: "Whenever I turned right or left on the Day of Uhud, I saw her fighting to defend me."

> *"Beware of shouting for it causes lethargy and avoid rudeness which is agony"*

---

¹ Surat an-Nisa', verse 81.

7

Piety towards man wipes away his pains

There are plenty of Hadiths of the Messenger of Allah, which praise the woman's generosity, whether in urging people to give charity, or their kindness or their preference of their friends or guests' happiness over their own.

'Aishah, the Mother of the believers, reported that they once slaughtered a sheep, so the Prophet 靐 said: "What is left of it?"
She replied: "Nothing is except its shoulder."
The Prophet 靐 said: "Everything is left, except its shoulder."

The Prophet 靐 explained to his family that whatever they gave in charity has its reward until the Day of Resurrection, and whatever left in this world and they have consumed, there would be no reward for it in the Hereafter. This is a noble hint, which urges people to give charity, seeking the pleasure of Allah 靐.

The Prophet 靐 advised Asma', the sister of 'Aishah 靐, to give charity, so that Allah 靐 would increase His blessings upon her; he 靐 said to her: "Do not withhold your money, for if you did so, Allah would withhold His blessings from you."

> *"As long as the night will end, the suffering will die down, the crisis will pass and hardship will vanish."*

"A blessing is a bribe with thankfulness as its dowry."

8
Turn your losses into gains

An advice says: "Do not despair if you tripped and you fell in a wide hole; you will come out of it with more determination and strength, for Allah ﷻ is with the patient.

Do not feel sad when you are struck by a lethal arrow from the closest person to your heart; for you will find someone who will remove that arrow and heal your wound, and help you regain your life and smile.

Do not stand thinking about a ruined place, especially if it has become inhabited by bats or ghosts. Look for the sound of a bird, coming from above, along with the light of a new dawn.

Do not look at papers whose colour has changed and letters that have faded. Its lines are lost between torment and isolation. You will discover that these lines are the best things that you have written, and that these papers are the last thing you will ever write. You should distinguish between the one who has put your lines between his eyes and the one who has thrown them in the air.

These lines were not casual beautiful words; rather they were emotions, which the heart has felt, letter by letter. They were the pulse of a person who carried them as a dream and felt their burning pain.

Do not be like the melancholy heron, which sings its most beautiful songs while it is bleeding; for nothing in this world deserves a single drop of your blood.

"Whoever plants the wind, cultivates the storm."

9
Loyalty is very precious; where are the loyal?

The Prophet Ayyub ﷺ was one of those who have a good knowledge about Allah ﷻ, who submits to His Decree and who is pleased with His Judgment. He suffered affliction in his body, wealth and children. Every spot in his body was hurting him, except his heart. He had nothing left in this world to help him overcome his illness, but his wife stayed loyal to him thanks to her belief in Allah and His Messenger.

She worked as a servant to earn some money in order to feed and serve her husband for a period of eighteen years. She would not leave him mornings or evenings except when she went to work as a servant to other people; then she would return to him.

As his suffering continued, he turned to invoke Allah ﷻ, the Most Merciful, saying:
⟨Great harm has afflicted me and you are the Most Merciful and the merciful⟩²

So Allah ﷻ responded to his supplication and accepted his call. He ﷻ ordered him to stand up and beat the ground with his feet. Prophet Ayyub ﷺ did what Allah ﷻ commanded him to do, and Allah caused water to come out from that

---

¹ Surat as-Saffat, verse 49.
² Surat al-Anbiya', Verse 83.

spot. He ﷻ commanded him to bath with it, and all the signs of his illness disappeared. Then He ﷻ commanded him to strike another spot on the ground and another spring of water gushed forth; He ﷻ then ordered him to drink from it, and all the harm in his stomach was removed.

His good health was accomplished both inside and outside of his body, and this was the result of being patient, of seeking only the reward of Allah ﷻ and of accepting His Decree.

"Man might regret saying a word, but will never regret being silent."

10
Be serious

Y ou should be serious in all your matters; in the upbringing of your children, in exercising a beneficial activity, in reading interesting books, in reciting the Qur'an, in offering a prayer, in remembering Allah ﷻ, in giving charity, in doing your housework or organising your bookshelves, so that you leave no room to worry and anxiety.

Look at the case of some disbelieving women – not to mention believing ones – and how they were distinguished with their serious attitude in life, despite their disbelief and misguidance. The ex-Prime Minister of Israel, the late Golda Mayer, left memoirs which described her seriousness, her organization of the army and her approach to the war against the Arabs. Only few men of her race did similar work, even though she was a disbeliever and an enemy of Allah!

> *"Happiness is not some kind of magic; had it been so, it would not have any value."*

CHAPTER 12

❲Truly, Allah is with those who fear Him and those who are good-doers❳[1]

1
Take a brave stand to account yourself

Ask yourself these questions and give reasonable answers:

- Do you know that you set out on a journey with no return? Have you prepared for it?
- Have you supplied yourself from this ending world with righteous deeds, which will comfort your loneliness in the grave?
- How old are you? How long will you live? Don't you know that everything has an end and that the end is either in Paradise or in Hell?
- Have you ever imagined the fact that the angels will come down from the heavens to take your soul, while you are careless?
- Have you thought of that last day and hour in your life; the hour when you leave your family, children and friends? It is death with its agonies and pains...

---

[1] Surat surat An-Nahl, Verse 128.

When your spirit leaves your body, you will be taken to be washed and shrouded, then to the mosque for your funeral, and immediately, you will carried on men's shoulders... but where is your final destination?

It is the grave: the first stopover to the hereafter. It is either one of the gardens of Paradise or one of the holes of Hell!

> *"Consider your failure a lesson to be learnt from"*

❰It is He who sends down the rain after they have despaired❱[1]

2
Beware!

Beware of assuming the manners of disbelieving and impudent women or men.
The Prophet ﷺ said: "Allah has cursed the women who assume the manners of men and has cursed the men who assume the manners of women."[2]

Beware of everything that earns the Anger of Allah ﷻ, as mentioned in the traditions of the Prophet ﷺ, such as adopting the manners of men, or staying alone with a male stranger, or travelling without the company of a mahram[3], or losing chastity, or displaying adornment and beauty, or forgetting your Lord.

These are all shameful deeds, which bring distress and misery to the heart in both this world and the Hereafter. Unfortunately, these acts have become widely spread among Muslim women, except those blessed by Allah ﷻ.

"In order to be beautiful, you need to have beautiful thinking."

---

[1] Surat Ash-Shura, Verse 28.
[2] Recorded by al-Bukhari.
[3] A man whom a woman cannot marry legally, such as her father, brother, son, etc.

⟨Our Lord, forgive us our sins and the excess in our affairs⟩[1]

3
It is a duty to be grateful to the beneficent

Al-Khyzaran was a slave woman whom the caliph, Al-Mahdi, had bought from a slave trader, and set free before he married her. He met her demands and appointed her parents as heirs, yet whenever she got angry, she would say in his face: "I have never witnessed anything good from you!"

Al-Barmakiyah was another slave woman, who was bought by Al-Mu'tamid ibn 'Abbad, the King of Al-Maghrib. He set her free and appointed her as queen. When she saw her servants playing with mud, she had a longing for her past and desired to play in the mud like them. So Al-Mu'tamid ordered for a great amount of perfume to be set up as mud for her to play with. She enjoyed herself playing with it; yet whenever she got angry with him, she would say: "I have never witnessed anything good from you!" and he would smile and reply to her: "Not even the day of the mud?" and she would get embarrassed and shy!

It is the nature of women, except a few of them, to forget any favour done to them, when they feel being carelessly neglected. It was reported that the Prophet ﷺ said: "O women, give charity, for I have seen that you make the majority of the dwellers of the Hell-fire." The women

---

[1] Surat al-'Imran, Verse 147.

185

replied: "Why is it so, O Messenger of Allah?" he ﷺ answered: "You curse frequently and are ungrateful to your husbands."

He ﷺ said: "I was shown the hell-Fire and most of its dwellers were women, because they were ungrateful to their husbands and to any beneficent act towards them. If you treat one of them well during all your life, and then she dislikes something from you, she would say: "I have never seen anything good from you!"

If a man knows the nature of a woman, he does not feel angry and does not lose his temper, when she is ungrateful to him, even if he has done a great deal for her.

"A successful woman mentioned in one's supplications, praised by her husband, loved by her neighbour and respected by her friends."

4
The soul has precedence in care over the body

When 'Umar ibn Abdul-Aziz was Caliph, he ordered a man to buy him a garment with eight dirhams. The man duly did so and brought it before him. 'Umar ran his hand over it and said: "What a soft and beautiful garment!" The man, who brought it smiled, and 'Umar asked him: "What made you smile?"

The man replied: "O Amir of the believers, you ordered me before you assumed the caliphate to buy you a coat made of the finest silk , and I bought it for you for a thousand dirhams, and when you put your hands on it you said: "How rough it is!" And now you find softness with a garment of eight dirhams!"

'Umar said: "I do not think a man who buys a garment for a thousand dirhams really fears Allah ﷻ" then he added: "I have a very ambitious soul. Whenever I reach a position, I aspire for a higher one. I became a governor, so I aspired for the caliphate. And now that I am a caliph, I long for what is even higher: Paradise."

"It is not our responsibility to judge people. We should not think about the punishment of others."

---

[1] Hadith Qudsi, a Hadith in which the Prophet ﷺ quotes Allah's Words.

"Be mindful of Allah, and He ﷻ will protect you."

5

Focus on the present rather than the past or the future

What is the point of slapping one's cheeks and tearing one's clothes in lament over a missed chance or bad luck? What benefit does a person get when he or she stands thinking about a painful past event?

Had it been in our hands to go back in time and change whatever we disliked of events and make them pleasant for us, then it would have been our duty to do so. We would all have rushed to the past and changed all our regrettable actions and increased our share of good deeds. But since it is impossible, it is better that we boost our efforts for the coming days and nights, in which there is a chance for compensation.

This is what was highlighted in the Qur'an, after the Battle of Uhud, when it addressed those who mourned the dead and who regretted going to the battlefield:

❨Say: Even if you had remained in your homes, those for whom death was decreed would certainly have gone forth to the place of their death.❩[1]

> *"Be certain that happiness is like the flower which has not yet blossomed, but its flowering is definite."*

---

[1] Surat al-'Imran, Verse 154.

{But whoever turns away from My Reminder, his life will be a dark and narrow one}[1]

6
Calamities are means of expiation and compensation

U mm Al'Ala', may Allah be pleased with her said: "The Messenger of Allah ﷺ visited me while I was sick. He said: 'Be glad, Umm Al-Ala', for Allah removes the sins of a Muslim; for his illness is as a fire that removes the dross of gold and silver.'"

This does not mean that we should let germs grow in our body and not treat them, on the pretext that illness wipes away sins. A sick person should seek recovery and use medicines, while he is being patient and seeking rewards only from Allah ﷻ. He should look at his pains as a means of accumulating good deeds in his record, and this is what the righteous woman has taught us.

A Woman should be patient when she loses a loved one, such a spouse or a child. The Prophet ﷺ said: "Allah ﷻ will not be pleased with any other reward for his believing slave other than Paradise, if when he loses a beloved person, he displays patience and seeks the reward of Allah."

If a woman loses her husband, then it is only that Allah ﷻ has taken back His slave, and He ﷻ is more entitled to have

---

[1] Surat Ta-Ha, Verse 124.

him. If the woman says: "It's my husband," or "It's my child!". Allah ﷻ, the Creator, says: "It's My slave, and I am more entitled to have him before anyone. A husband is a loan; a child is a loan; a brother is a loan; a father is a loan; a wife is a loan."

"Keep away from insults, just as you keep away from the plague."

7

Be merciful to those on earth, and you will be shown mercy by those in heaven

The Mercy of the mother upon her children is well mentioned in the Hadiths of the Prophet 繼. It is the example of love and affection, and the source of care and compassion. Allah 繼 has created her as a spring, which overflows with love towards her children. The Prophet 繼 used a real-life scenario to explain the Mercy of Allah 繼 upon His slaves.

'Umar ibn Al-Khattab 繼, the Amir of the believers, said: "Some women taken after a battle were brought to the Messenger of Allah 繼. One of them was walking around searching for something, then when she saw a little boy, she hugged him closely against her chest and started breastfeeding him. The Messenger of Allah 繼 said: 'Can you imagine this woman throwing her child onto the fire?' we said: "No, by Allah." So he 繼 said: "Verily, Allah is more Merciful to His slaves than this woman is to her child."

This woman was captured and taken after a battle; she was sad and very upset. She was a respected lady in her family and tribe, free among the men of her clan, obeyed in her marital home, but her captivity after the battle had made her a serving slave-girl. This is very difficult mental situation, which makes one lose his mind and his heart out of agony.

But this calamity did not distract her thinking about her child. She looked for him everywhere until she found and hugged him affectionately, before she breastfed him.

A woman like this one would never allow harm to reach her child, whatever his age; she would never let him be hurt, and would protect him with herself against all evil.

> *"Evil tongues bring more damage to their own people than to their victims."*

8
The beautiful world is seen only by the optimist

If winter has forced you to stay indoors, as mountains of snow besiege you from everywhere, then look forward to spring to open your windows for fresh air. Look far ahead and you will see flocks of birds singing; you will witness the sun's warming rays above the branches to give you a new life, a new dream and a new heart.

Do not travel to the desert looking for beautiful trees. You will find only loneliness there. Look at the hundreds of trees, which embrace you with their shade, delight you with their fruits, and move your heart with its birdsongs.

Do not try to redo whatever happened yesterday and what you have lost in it; for when a leaf falls from its tree, it will never go back to its previous place. However, there are other leaves with every new spring. Therefore, look at the leaves up in the sky and ignore those fallen on the ground, for they have become part of it.

If yesterday was lost, you have today between your hands. If today will collect its leaves and disappear, then you have tomorrow ahead. Do not grieve over yesterday, for it will not come back and do not feel sad about today, for it is leaving; but dream of a shining sun for a beautiful tomorrow.

"It is not possible to imagine the extent of sickness generated by the exchange of hurtful words."

9
Get to know Allah in prosperity and He will know you in adversity

When Prophet Yunus ﷺ felt distressed inside the belly of the whale, surrounded by the darkness of the sea, the darkness inside the big fish and the darkness of the night, he was distraught and extremely worried, so he turned to Allah ﷻ, the One with the salvation for the depressed and the refuge for the miserable, the One who accepts sincere repentance of His slaves, as His Mercy embraces everything in this life. Yunus ﷺ invoked Allah ﷻ saying:

{He called out in the darkness: "There is no god but You! Glory be to You! Truly I have been one of the wrongdoers"}[1]

The quick reply came, as Allah ﷻ said:

{We responded to him and rescued him from his grief. That is how We rescue the believers}[2]

Allah ﷻ inspired the whale to throw Yunus ﷺ outside, so he came out to the shore very ill and weak. Allah ﷻ took him in His Care and Mercy; so He ﷻ caused a tree with

---

[1] Surat al-Anbiya', Verse 87.
[2] Surat al-Anbiya', Verse 88.

broad leaves to grow around him. He gradually regained his health, as signs of life appeared on him.

As the Prophet ﷺ said: "Get to know Allah ﷻ in prosperity and He will know you in adversity."

"It is impossible to be fit to lead yourself, until you deserve to lead your life."

10

The woman with the most expensive dowry in the world

Abu Talhah proposed to marry Umm Sulaym ibn Milhan, offering her a very expensive dowry, but he was astonishingly surprised and dumbfounded when Umm Sulaym refused his proposal, and said proudly and defiantly: "I should not marry a disbeliever. Don't you know, O Abu Talhah that your gods are carved by the slave of so and so, and that if you put fire to them, they will burn?"

Abu Talhah felt very distressed, so he left while he hardly believed what he saw and heard. However, his sincere love made him come back the following day, offering her a greater dowry and more comfortable life, in the hope that she might accept. She replied with utmost courtesy: "A man of your rank is not to be refused, O Abu Talhah, but you are a disbeliever, and I am a Muslim woman. It is not right for me to marry you."

So he said: "That was not your dowry." She asked what is my dowry then?" he said: "The yellow and the white (gold and silver)." She said: "I neither want the yellow nor the white. I want you to embrace Islam." He said: "Who can show me the way?" she said: "The Messenger of Allah." So he went to look for the Prophet ﷺ, who was sitting with his Companions. When the Prophet ﷺ saw him, he said: "Abu Talhah has come to you with the light of Islam in his eyes."

Abu Talhah informed the Prophet ﷺ about what Umm Sulaym has said to him, and so he married her in Islam.

This woman is a great example for every woman who seeks glory and virtue. Look at the way she gave signs of nobility and faith with her good biography. Look at the value of her reward with Allah ﷻ, which was the result of her sincerity with her Lord, with herself and with people.

Allah ﷻ says: ❨**This is a Day on which the truthful will profit from their truthfulness**❩[1]

She has deservingly earned a great reward, an entry to Paradise, to abide in timelessly.

> *"You need to smile if you want others to smile at you"*

---

[1] Surat al-Ma'idah, Verse 119.

CHAPTER 13

⟨Bear with patience whatever befalls you⟩[1]

1
The keys to victory

- The key to glory: Obedience to Allah and His Messenger.

- The key to provision: Striving while seeking Allah's Forgiveness and being mindful of Him.

- The key to Paradise: belief in the Oneness of Allah ﷻ.

- The key to faith: Pondering on Allah's Signs and Creation.

- The key to righteousness: Truthfulness.

- The key to a living heart: Understanding the meaning of the Qur'an, invoking Allah's Mercy in hours before dawn, and giving up sins.

- The key to knowledge: asking right questions and listening carefully.

- The key to victory: Patience.

- The key to success: Piety and fear of Allah.

---

[1] Surat Luqman, Verse 17.

- The key to increased blessings: Gratitude

- The key to the longing for the Hereafter: Disinterest in this world's commodities.

- The key to a response: Supplication.

"A smile is a beam of sunshine."

2
There is delight of victory after a period of agony

After spending her honeymoon, a newlywed woman wrote to her mother, saying: "Dear mother, today I returned home – our little nest – which was prepared by my husband, after we have spent our honeymoon. I really wanted you to be near me, O mother… to tell you everything of my experience in my new life with my husband. He is such a good man who loves me and I love him. I do everything I can to please him. Be assured, O mother, that I keep your instructions and I do exactly as you advised me. I still remember every word and every letter you have told me or whispered in my ear, while you hugged me on my wedding night. I see life the way you see it, as you are my great example. I have no goal except to do exactly what you have done with my good father and with us, your children. You have given us all your love and affection. You have taught us the meaning of life and how to live it, and you have planted the seeds of love in our hearts.

I hear the key turning inside the lock, it must be my husband. He wants to read my letter to you, he wants to know what I write to my mother. He wants to share with me these happy moments, which I spent with you in spirit and thought. He

---

[1] Surat al-'Imran. Verse 8.

asks me to let him write something to you. I send my love to you, to my father and to my brothers and sisters.
Goodbye.

"A smile does not cost anything, but gives a great deal in return."

3
Anxiety torments the mind and body

One of the worst features of anxiety is that it weakens the ability to concentrate. When we are worried, our mind is scattered; but when we commit ourselves to face up to worst scenarios, we then put ourselves in a situation where we force our mind to focus on the core of the problem.

It is not in our ability to get excited for a particular activity, while we are still worried; for one of these two feelings – excitement and worry – will chase the other away.

If you feel anxious about the present, then think back of the worst case of worry, which you have suffered in the past. Thus, your mind will deal with two different kinds of worry instead of one, and the worst case of past will prevail over the present one which is less critical. It is then when a person says: "There is nothing that could be worse than the past case, which I managed to overcome successfully and safely.

Anxiety is more likely to control your mind in your free time and not in your work time; because then your mind is roaming in imagination, which attracts all sorts of

---

[1] Surat al-Baqarah, Verse 127.

assumptions and possible scenarios. The only remedy for these is to keep yourself busy with a serious activity.

"Silly things may sometimes push wisest people to the brink of insanity."

4
Your loved activity is the secret of your happiness

An ingenious person in any field is guided irresistibly towards the field, which Allah ﷻ has created him and induced him with the skills for. If he complains for his bad luck of being in that field, then he should know that it is the only activity which he may practise with delight.

Despite all the difficulties which he may face in his activity, wishing he could leave it for another job, or complaining about his poverty which forced him into it, he should know that his present activity is the only one now which provides him with contentment and brings the best out of him.

"The happiness of a man is in a word which comes out from the mouth of a woman."

5
Power is in one's heart not in his body

A Christian woman had known little in life except sickness, sorrow and tragedy. Her husband had died shortly after their marriage. Her second husband had deserted her and eloped with a married woman. He later died in poverty. She had one child, a son; and she was forced because of poverty and illness, to give him up when he was four years old.

The dramatic turning point in her life occurred when she was walking downtown; she slipped and fell on the icy pavement, and was knocked unconscious for a long period of time. She sustained a serious spinal injury in her fall. Doctors expected that she would either die almost immediately or suffer paralysis for the rest of her life.

Lying on what was supposed to be her deathbed, she opened her Bible, and was led, she declared, by divine guidance to read these words from Saint Mathew: "And, behold, they brought to him (i.e. Jesus ﷺ) a man sick of the palsy, lying on a bed, and he said to him: son, arise, take up thy bed, and go unto thine house and he arose and went to his house."

These words produced within her such a strength, such a faith, such a surge of healing power, that she immediately got out of bed and walked in her room! "That experience,"

---

[1] Surat Ash-Shu'ara', Verse 80.

Mrs Eddy declared, "was the falling apple that led me to the discovery of how to be well myself, and how to make others so."

Dale Carnegie said: "Such is the way in which Mary Baker Eddy became the founder and high priestess of a new religion: Christian Science – the only religious faith even established by a woman!"

And you dear Muslim sister, what have you done?

"The strongest fortress is a righteous woman"

6
A great woman turns misfortunes into cheerful events

The great female companion, Umm Sulaym, the wife of Abu Talhah ☀, was a fine example of patience over the loss of a child; so Allah ☀ compensated her greatly.

Anas ibn Malik ☀ narrated: Abu Talha had a child who was sick. Once, while Abu Talha was out, the child died. When Abu Talha returned home, he asked: "How is my son?" Umm Salaym (his wife) replied: "He is quieter than he has ever been." Then she brought supper for him and he took his supper and slept with her. When he had finished, she said to him, "Bury the child (as he's dead)."

Next morning, Abu Talhah came to the Messenger of Allah and told him about that. The Prophet ☀ said: "Did you sleep with your wife last night?" Abu Talhah said: "Yes". The Prophet ☀ said: "O Allah! Bestow your blessing on them as regards that night of theirs."

Umm Sulaim gave birth to a boy. Then Abu Talha took the child to the Prophet and Umm Sulaym sent some dates along with the child. The Prophet took the child (on his lap) and asked if there was something with him. The people replied: "Yes, a few dates." The Prophet took a date, chewed it, took some of it out of his mouth, put it into the child's mouth and did Tahnik for him with that, and named him 'Abdullah.

"Nothing raises the status of a woman like chastity"

7
Be patient to prevail

It is narrated that Umm ar-Rubay bint Al-Bara', the mother of Harithah ibn Suraqah who was killed in the battle of Uhud, came to the Prophet ﷺ hoping to hear something from him, regarding her martyred son, that would appease her heart. She said: "O Messenger of Allah, would you tell something about Harithah; if he is in Paradise, I'll be patient, and if he is not then I'll weep over his death."

The Prophet ﷺ replied: "There are many paradises and he is in the highest one, the Firdous."

The loss of a child is a serious matter, which tears the heart, but this woman asked the Prophet ﷺ only if her son was in Paradise so that she would meet him. Her patience over the death of her son raised her rank and that of her son in Paradise.

If her son was not to be in Paradise, then she would weep bitterly over his loss, and that was all she could do, for she was bereaved of her child, and was merciful and patient.

> *"If a beautiful woman is a jewel, then a righteous woman is a treasure."*

8
We only have Allah ﷻ to turn to in hardship

When anxiety settles in and worry takes over one's mind, and he feels helpless in his misfortune or hardship, he cries out: "O Allah! O Allah! There is no god but Allah, The Almighty and The Ever-Forbearing. There is no god but Allah, The Lord of the Mighty Throne. There is no god but Allah, The Lord of the heavens and earth, The Lord of the Noble Throne." Then he feels relieved of his worry and distress.

Allah ﷻ says:

❨So We answered his call, and delivered him from the distress. Thus We do deliver the believers❩[1]
❨Whatever of blessings and good things you have, it is from Allah. Then, when harm touches you, to Him you cry aloud for help❩[2]

When the state of the sick worsens, his body becomes weak, his face turns pale, and his doctor is helpless to cure his illness, he turns to the Almighty Allah: "O Allah! O Allah!" then he becomes relieved of his pain, as his healing takes place. His supplication was answered:

---

[1] Surat al-Anbiya', Verse 88.
[2] Surat an-Nahl, Verse 53.

211

❨...and Ayyub, when he cried to his Lord: "Verily, distress has seized me, and You are the Most Merciful of all those who show mercy." So We answered his call, and We removed the distress that was on him, and We restored his family to him and the like thereof along with them as a mercy from Ourselves and a Reminder for all those who worship Us.❩[1]

> *"The best thing that a man can have is a loyal wife."*

---

[1] Surat al-Anbiya', Verses 83-84.

9

He who responds to the oppressed when they call on him

It is out of Allah's Generosity that He ﷻ does not let down the one who calls on him. The relief or the response to the supplication comes according to one's need and submissiveness before Allah ﷻ.

It is out of Allah's Generosity also to answer the call of non-Muslims, when they turn to him, in humility, as they trust His Kindness and hope for His Bounty. He ﷻ answers their call and removes their distress, in case they might believe. But most people ignore His Merit upon them and are ungrateful to Him; He ﷻ says:

❮When they embark on a ship, they invoke Allah, making their faith pure for Him only; but when brings them safely to land, behold, they give a share of their worship to others.❯[1]

Allah ﷻ reminds His slaves that He is the One Who answers the oppressed and relieves him of his agony. That is one Sign of His Deity and a proof of Oneness, but only few people remember. He ﷻ says:

---

[1] Surat al-Ankabut, Verse 65.

⟨He who responds to the oppressed when they call on him, and removes their distress, and has appointed you as inheritors on the earth. Is there another god besides Allah? No, indeed; But most of them do not know⟩[1]

> *"A Woman should stay in her house, because she is like a fragile vessel, which can break easily"*

---

[1] Surat an-Naml, Verse 62.

10

❧Whoever is tight-fisted is only tight-fisted to himself❧[1]

A famous narration about Umm Al-Banin, daughter of Abdul-'Aziz – the sister of 'Umar ibn Abdul-'Aziz – and her generosity reported that she used to invite people in her house, dress them with fine clothes and offer them money, before she would say to them: "The clothes are yours and the money I divide it among you poor ones."

She intended thereby to teach them to spend in charity and be generous. She was quoted as saying: "By Allah, if miserliness were a piece of cloth I would not wear it, and if it were a road, I would never take it."

Among her famous quotes, regarding generosity: "Everyone is naturally craving for something, and my craving is directed only to giving charity and helping other people. By Allah, keeping good kinship and consoling others is more loved to me than a good meal when I am hungry or a cold drink when I am thirsty."

Because of her keenness to give charity and to spend money properly, she used to say: "I have never envied anyone for something, except when someone does favours to others for

---

[1] Surat Muhammad, Verse 38.

the sake of Allah; for I would like to share such a good deed."

This was Umm Al-Banin, and these were her words and actions. But where are the likes of Umm Al-Banin?

"In the elimination of selfishness lies true happiness"

CHAPTER 14

⟨Only those who are patient shall receive their reward in full, without reckoning⟩[1]

1
You are a Muslim woman, neither eastern nor western

This is an advice from a German Muslim woman: Do not be deceived with the west and its ideas and fashions. It is but a trap to mislead us gradually away from our religion, in order to seize our wealth.

Islam and its family system is the one which suits women, because it is in her nature to stay in the house, but you may ask why?

Because Allah ﷻ has created men as more powerful than women, in their endurance, intellect and physical power; and He ﷻ created women as sensitive and more emotional; they do not have the physical strength of men. Their character is to a certain extent unstable than that of men; therefore, the house is their abode.

The woman who loves her husband and children does not leave her house without any reason, and definitely does not mix with other men.

---

[1] Surat az-Zumar, Verse 10.

Ninety percent of women in the west have not reached their degrading state, until they have sold themselves, as there is no fear of Allah in their hearts.

When women went out to work in the western world in this intense manner, men were forced to perform the role of women; so they stayed home washing dishes, looking after the children and drinking alcohol.

I know that Islam does not forbid a man from helping his wife at home; it rather encourages it, but not to the extent where roles are reversed.

"Be beautiful and you will see the world as beautiful"

2

Forget your worries and focus on your work

If you do not know what you should do to solve a particular problem, then distract yourself away from it with a hobby, reading or any activity. Activity takes the place of worry in this case. Allah ﷻ has not made for any man two hearts inside his body. Let's suppose that the problem is the illness of a child; here the parents do everything they could to cure him, and then they go to their work.

It is advisable for a person who endures such a problem to remember past difficult problems, especially those bigger crises, and how Allah ﷻ has helped him overcome them, until they became memories of a confident mind. When a person thinks in this manner, he feels that today's problem will pass and be solved like the previous ones. By Allah's Will, it will be history.

A person should seek the positive side of his problem, and realise that they certainly could be worse than they actually are. Ibn Al-Juzy said: "Whoever is afflicted by a calamity should imagine it worse than it is and it will sound easy for him; he should think of its rewards. He should think of worse calamities, which would make him accept the present one. He should look forward to its quick end; indeed

---

[1] Surat al-A'la, Verse 8.

without critical hardships, there would not be such a longing for relief."

"A wise man said: I never regretted what I have not said, but I have very much regretted what I did say."

3
Some ideas to help you achieve happiness

A varice and greed are deadly characters; their remedy is as follow:

1- Cut down your expenses and avoid spending freely, for whoever expands his spending, he will never meet self-satisfaction; he will rather be a victim of his own greed. Economy of one's living is the basis of contentment. Indeed, the saying goes: "Good management saves half one's income."

2- Do not worry too much about the future; build your hopes on only the short term and the belief that the provision decreed for you will definitely reach you.

3- Fear Allah and be mindful of Him in all your activities; for He ﷻ says:
⟨**Whosoever fears Allah, He will make a way out for him, and He will provide him from sources he never could imagine.**⟩[2]

4- Know that there is pride in contentment and disgrace in greed and avarice, and learn a lesson in that.

---

[1] Surat al-'Imran, Verse 8.
[2] Surat at-Talaq, Verses 2-3.

5- Think often of the conditions of Prophets and righteous men, their contentment and moderation in life and their desire for righteous deeds.

6- Look at those less fortunate than you in worldly matters.

> *"A reasonable person does not despair and does not give up striving."*

4
Build up a strong link with Allah when other links fail

The righteous deed, together with faith is rewarded with a good life on the earth. It is not important if it is a life in luxury and wealth; for a blessed life can be attained with or without material wealth.

There are many other things which make life good, apart from ample wealth, to the limit of sufficiency, such as: A relationship with Allah ﷻ, the trust in Him ﷻ, the belief in His Care and Pleasure. Good health, tranquillity, peace at home and mutual affections.The joy of doing righteous deeds and their effects on one's mind and life in general.

Money remains just one aspect, a little of which is enough so that the heart is linked with what is greater, purer and lasting in the sight of Allah.

> *"It is an established theory that great men inherit the characteristics of their greatness from their mothers."*

---

[1] Surat al-Hajj, Verse 38.

5
No one is happier than those who believe in Allah

I have read the biographies of many wealthy and great personalities of the world, who did not believe in Allah ﷻ, and found that their lives ended in misery, their future in Allah's Curse and their glory in disgrace.

Where are they now? Where is the wealth which they gathered and the palaces and mansions which they built? It has all come to an end!

Some of them committed suicide, some were assassinated, others were imprisoned, and the rest were taken to courts, as a punishment of their crimes and offences.

They became the most miserable of people. They once thought that money could buy everything for them, such as happiness, love, good health and youth. Then, they realised that true happiness, true love, good health and true youth cannot be bought with money!

Yes, they can buy, from the market, illusive happiness, false love and deceptive health, but all the money of the world cannot buy a heart, plant pure love or create peace of mind.

---

[1] Surat an-Nahl, Verse 35.

No one is happier that the believers in Allah ﷻ, because they are under the light of their Lord. They subject themselves to account; they enjoin Allah's Command and avoid His Prohibitions. Allah ﷻ says to them:

❨**Whoever does righteousness – whether male or female – while he (she) is a believer in Allah, verily, to him We will give a good life, and We shall pay them certainly a reward in proportion to the best of what they used to do**❩[1]

> *"He is not happy, who does not want to be happy."*

---

[1] Surat an-Nahl, Verse 97.

6
A life without extravagance or lavishness

The righteous Muslim woman prepares food according to need. No food is left on the table which denotes her extravagance and ill-management. Her example (to follow) is the Mother of the believers, 'Aishah 🌸, who said: "No barley bread used to be left on the dinner table of the Messenger of Allah, whether little or plenty."

In another narration, she was quoted as saying: "There was never a dinner table cleared away before the Messenger of Allah, while there was extra food on it."

Islam has forbidden the use of silver or golden meal utensils, as they are considered as part of extravagance in life. Umm Salamah 🌸 said: "The Messenger of Allah 🌸 said: 'The one who drinks in silver vessels is actually swallowing the hellfire in his stomach."

The truth is that Islam is ever wise in this prohibition; for such things are among luxuries, and they are signs of the extravagant. Islam recommends that its followers be modest and non-extravagant.

The Prophet 🌸 said to Mu'adh ibn Jabal when he 🌸 sent him to Yemen: "Beware of luxury, for the slaves of Allah are not those who live in luxury."

> *"When you abstain from looking at your inner misery, you will be happy."*

7
Good deeds bring delight and satisfaction

'Aishah, may Allah be pleased with said: "A poor woman with her two daughters came to me asking for some alms and I gave each of them a date. When the woman wanted to eat hers, her daughters asked for more, so she divided her date between the two of them. I was impressed by her act, so I mentioned it to the Prophet 鐵, and he 鐵 said: "Allah 鐵 has commended for her entry to Paradise or salvation from the hellfire."

Umm Salamah, may Allah be pleased with her, asked the Prophet 鐵 regarding her spending on her children, saying: "Shall I be rewarded when I spend on the children of Abu Salamah, as I am not going to neglect them, since they are my children as well?"

She admitted that she would never neglect them, before the Prophet 鐵 gave a positive answer. In fact, instinctive nature had answered her before his answer.

Indeed, it is Islam which urges the performance of righteous deeds and good actions, to show compassion with one's relatives, and introduce mercy and love in society, so that our children are brought righteously.

> *"Be happy... there is here the true happiness!"*

8
May Allah safeguard us from every trouble

When a plane flies at high altitude and its indicator points to a technical failure, and signs of malfunction appear, the pilot is worried, the passengers are terrified, and the place becomes noisy, as men, women and children are weeping. There is frightening panic as everyone is scared and unsettled; so they turn to invoke Allah: Oh Allah, Oh Allah, Oh Allah. Then Allah's Kindness reaches them and His Mercy embraces them, to allow their hearts and their souls to become cool, calm and collected, as the plane lands in peace.

When a baby becomes hard to deliver and his mother is on the brink of death, she turns to Allah ﷻ, The One Who relieves from distress and meets His slaves' needs, yelling: "Oh Allah, Oh Allah, Oh Allah" and then her moaning ceases and her baby is born safely to this world.

When a scholar faces a difficulty and is confused about a particular matter, and cannot find the answer to it, he rubs his nose on the ground, in submissive prostration, saying: "Oh Allah, Oh Allah, Oh Teacher of Ibrahim, teach me! You made Sulayman understand, so help me understand. Oh Allah, Lord of Jibril, Mickael, Israfil, Creator of the heavens and earth, Knower of the unseen and the seen world, You judge between Your slaves concerning that wherein they differ, guide me to the truth concerning that wherein they differ by Your Leave; for You guide whomsoever You want to the Straight Path" Then the relief and success comes from Him, the All Merciful, Glory to Him ﷻ.

"The happiest person is the one who helps make many people happy"

9
Beware of negligence

Beware of negligence; it is laxity regarding the remembrance of Allah 🕮, abstention from performing Salat, turning away from the Qur'an, ignoring lectures and beneficial lessons. These are some of the reasons of negligence, which toughens the heart and places a seal on it, until it no longer recognises a righteous deed, or reproaches a bad one. The person's heart becomes insensitive and hard, and these are the consequences of negligence in this world, so what about the Hereafter!

Therefore, you have to avoid the causes of negligence. Fear Allah; always keep your tongue fresh with the remembrance of Allah 🕮, saying:
Subhanallah (Glory to Allah)
La ilaha illa Allah (There is no god but Allah)
Allah-u-Akbar (Allah is the Greatest)
al-Hamdu-lillah (Praise to Allah)
Astaghfiru Allah (I ask Allah for forgiveness)
Allahumma salli wa sallim 'ala Muhammad (Allah's Peace and Prayer upon Muhammad)

You repeat these words all the time, when you are standing or sitting or lying on your side. It is then you will witness happiness embracing you, and this is the outcome of the remembrance of Allah, as He 🕮 says:

❬Verily, in the remembrance of Allah do hearts find rest❭[1]

"Do not wait until you are happy so that you smile, but smile to be happy!"

---

[1] Surat ar-Ra'd, Verse 28.

10
Smile at life

When you smile and your heart is full of worries, you lessen your suffering and open a door for your relief. Do not hesitate to smile, for there is inside a lot of energy to be cheerful; so do not restrain it, because you would then strangle yourself with pain and agony.

It will not hurt you to smile, to talk to others with cheerfulness. How wonderful it is when our lips speak with the language of smiles!

Stephen Jezel said: "A smile is a social obligation" and he was right, because when you intend to meet people, you have to socialise with them nicely, and you have to understand that social life requires from you some human potentials which you should master. Among these skills, a smile is a social common fact among people.

When you smile in the face of others, you provide them with the beauty of life and the spirit of optimism; but when you face them with a merciless face, you make them suffer with that image and disturb their life.

So why would accept to be the cause of the misery of other people's lives?

"Glory is granted only to those who have always dreamed of it."

CONCLUSION

And Now...

After reading this book, say farewell to sorrow, give up worrying, and leave all aspects of depression.

Desert all places of despair and frustration.

Come to the platform of faith, the stage of Allah's Comfort, the place to accept His Divine Decree, in order to start a new life, but a happy one, to start different days but pleasant ones.

Come to start a life with no hesitation, worry, confusion, boredom or despair.

It is then when the caller of faith calls you from above the mountain of hope, to announce the glad tidings:

"You are the happiest woman in the world!"

£7.95

تفسير
القرآن العظيم

TAFSIR
IBN KATHIR

PART 1

Surah Al-Fatiah
Surah Al-Baqarah 1 to 141

ABRIDGED BY
Sheikh Muḥammad Nasib Ar-Rafa'i

Al-Firdous Ltd., London

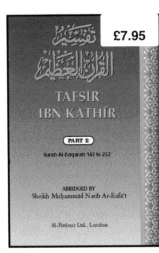

£7.95

تفسير
القرآن العظيم

TAFSIR
IBN KATHIR

PART 2

Surah Al-Baqarah 142 to 252

ABRIDGED BY
Sheikh Muḥammad Nasib Ar-Rafa'i

Al-Firdous Ltd., London

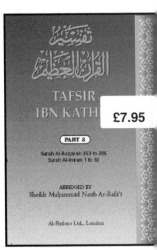

£7.95

تفسير
القرآن العظيم

TAFSIR
IBN KATHIR

£7.95

PART 3

Surah Al-Baqarah 253 to 286
Surah Al-Imran 1 to 92

ABRIDGED BY
Sheikh Muḥammad Nasib Ar-Rafa'i

Al-Firdous Ltd., London

تفسير
القرآن العظيم

TAFSIR
IBN KATHIR

PART 4

£7.95

Surah Al-Imran, ayat 93 to 200
Surah An-Nisa, ayat 1 to 23

ABRIDGED BY
Sheikh Muhammad Nasib Ar-Rafa'i

Al-Firdous Ltd., London

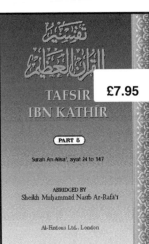

تفسير
القرآن العظيم

TAFSIR £7.95
IBN KATHIR

PART 5

Surah An-Nisa', ayat 24 to 147

ABRIDGED BY
Sheikh Muḥammad Nasib Ar-Rafa'i

Al-Firdous Ltd., London

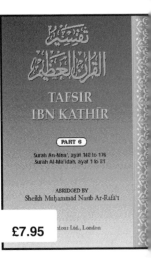

تفسير
القرآن العظيم

TAFSIR
IBN KATHIR

PART 6

Surah An-Nisa', ayat 148 to 176
Surah Al-Ma'idah, ayat 1 to 81

ABRIDGED BY
Sheikh Muḥammad Nasib Ar-Rafa'i

£7.95   dous Ltd., London

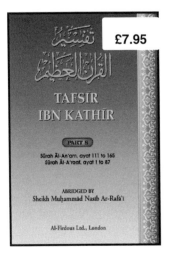

£7.95

تفسير
القرآن العظيم

TAFSIR
IBN KATHIR

PART 8

Sūrah Al-An'am, ayat 111 to 165
Sūrah Al-A'raaf, ayat 1 to 87

ABRIDGED BY
Sheikh Muḥammad Nasib Ar-Rafa'i

Al-Firdous Ltd., London

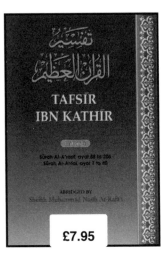

تفسير
القرآن العظيم

TAFSIR
IBN KATHIR

PART 7

Sūrah Al-A'raaf, ayat 88 to 206
Sūrah Al-Anfal, ayat 1 to 40

ABRIDGED BY
Sheikh Muḥammad Nasib Ar-Rafa'i

£7.95

تفسير
القرآن العظيم

TAFSIR
IBN KATHIR

£7.95

PART 10

Surah Al-Anfal 41 to 75
Surah Al-Tawbah 1 to 92

ABRIDGED BY
Sheikh Muḥammad Nasib Ar-Rafa'i

Al-Firdous Ltd., London

grief & depression

from an Islamic Perspective

Dr Abdullah al-Khater

£2.75

Winning *the* Heart *of your* Wife

Prepared by Saaleh al-Mahmud

£2.75

Winning *the* Heart *of your* Husband

Ibraahim ibn Saaleh al-Mahmud

£2.75

Al-Wala' Wa'l-Bara'

According to the 'Aqeedah of the Salaf

PART 1

Muhammad Saeed al-Qahtani

£3.95

Al-Wala' Wa'l-Bara'

According to the 'Aqeedah of the Salaf

PART 2

Muhammad Saeed al-Qahtani

£5.95

Al-Wala' Wa'l-Bara'

According to the 'Aqeedah of the Salaf

PART 3

Muhammad Saeed al-Qahtani

Al-Firdous Ltd., London

£4.95

SINCERE REPENTANCE

Imam Abu Hamid Ghazali
Imam Ibn Qayim Jawziya
Imam Ibn Rajab Hanbali

Al-Firdous Ltd., London

£2.50

FEAR OF ALLAH

In the light of the Quran, the Sunnah and the predecessors

Imam Ghazali, Imam Ibn Qayyim and Ibn Rajab Hanbali

Al-Firdous Ltd, London

£2.50

THE INGREDIENTS FOR A HAPPY MARRIAGE

Sheikh Nasir Al-Omar

Al-Firdous Ltd, London

£2.75

£3.95

The Purification of the Soul

£4.95

compiled from the works of
Ibn Rajab al-Hanbali, Ibn al-Qayyim al-Jawziyya,
and Abu Hamid al-Ghazali

TAQWA : THE PROVISION OF BELIEVERS

£2.50

Al-Firdous Ltd, London

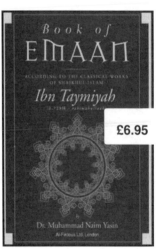

Book of
EMAAN

ACCORDING TO THE CLASSICAL WORKS
OF SHAIKHUL-ISLAM
Ibn Taymiyah

£6.95

Dr. Muhammad Naim Yasin
Al-Firdous Ltd, London

HEALING
OF THE **HEART**

£4.95

DR. MUHAMMED AZ-AZAHRANI

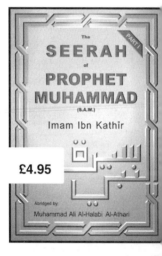

The
SEERAH
of
PROPHET MUHAMMAD
(S.A.W.)

Imam Ibn Kathīr

£4.95

Abridged by:
Muhammad Ali Al-Halabi Al-Athari

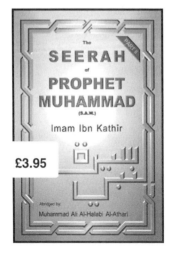

The
SEERAH
of
PROPHET MUHAMMAD
(S.A.W.)

Imam Ibn Kathīr

£3.95

Abridged by:
Muhammad Ali Al-Halabi Al-Athari

DAJJAL THE FALSE MESSIAH

£2.75

IMAM IBN KATHEER

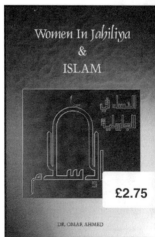

Women In Jahiliya
&
ISLAM

£2.75

DR. OMAR AHMED

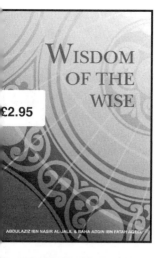

WISDOM OF THE WISE

£2.95

ABDULAZIZ IBN NASIR AL-JALIL & BAHA ADDIN IBN FATAH AQEEL

BACKBITING THE WAY TO HELLFIRE

£2.50

WAHEED ABDUSSALAAM BALY

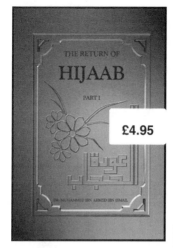

THE RETURN OF HIJAAB PART I

£4.95

THE RETURN OF HIJAAB PART II

£3.95

THE RETURN OF HIJAAB PART III

£4.95

TEN FRIGHTENNING THINGS FOR WOMEN

£2.75

ABU MARYAM MAJDI FATHI AL-SYED

Overcoming the fear of death & illness

£2.95

Dr. Muhammad Abu Rahim

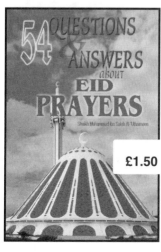

54 QUESTIONS & ANSWERS about EID PRAYERS

Sheikh Muhammad ibn Salih Al-Uthaimeen

£1.50

Authentic Interpretation of the DREAMS

According to Quraan & Sunnah

£3.95

Dr. Ahmed Fareed

Sword Against Black Magic & Evil Magicians

£5.95

WAHID ABDUSSALAM BALI

HOW TO BRING UP YOUR CHILDREN ISLAMICALLY

£2.75

WAHID ABDUSSALAM BALI

WASWASAH

The Whispering Of The SHAITAN

Al-Mu'aw

£3.50

Imam Ibn Qayyim Al-Juziyyah
Muwafaq Deen bin Qudaam Al-Hanbali

DESCRIPTION OF PARADISE

FROM THE QUR'AAN AUTHENTIC SUNNAH

£2.95

WAHEED ABDUSSALAAM BALI

30 Ways To Achieve HAPPINESS

£2.95

Aidh Ibn Abdullah Al-Qarni

TIME IS RUNNING OUT

£5.95

CATASTROPHES BEFORE THE DAY OF JUDGEMENT

IMAM SIDDIQ HASSAN KHAN

Winning the Heart of your Wife

£2.75

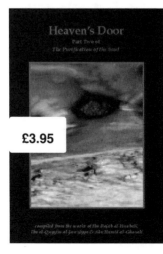

Heaven's Door
Part Two of
The Purification of the Soul

£3.95

STOP worrying

£6.95

relax & be HAPPY

Sheikh Muhammad Al-Gazali

PATIENCE & GOOD MANNERS

£5.95

AMR KHALID

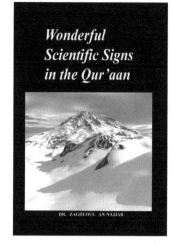

Wonderful Scientific Signs in the Qur'aan

DR. ZAGHLOUL AN-NAJJAR

OPPRESSION AND THE OPPRESSORS

£4.50

HOW TO ACHIEVE SINCERITY

£3.50

HUSSEIN AL-AWAYASHA

TAFSEER AL-MU'AWWIDHATAYN

Explanation of
Surah al-Falaq
Surah an-Nas

£3.95

IBN AL-QAYYIM AL-JAWZIYAH

£4.95

Lawful Wives Or Unlawful Girlfriends

POLYGAMY

KHASHI' HAQQI

HOW TO PROTECT YOURSELF FROM

JINN & SHAYTAN

£7.95

WAHEED ABDUSSALAM BALY

£2.75

Beware of Dajjal and Gog and Magog

MAGDY M. AL-SHAHAWI

STUDIES IN HADITH LITERATURE WITH A COMPLETE HADITH TERMINOLOGY

OMAR AHMED KASIR

£3.95

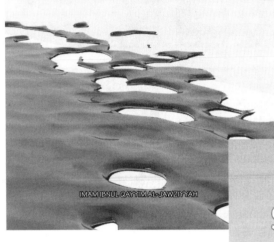

SPIRITUAL DISEASE AND IT'S CURE

IMAM IBNUL QAYYIM AL-JAWZIYYAH

FORTY SOLUTIONS TO YOUR MARRIAGE PROBLEMS

39
37 38 40

MUHAMMAD SALIH AL-MUNAJJID